Michael Krieger's Gripping Account of One of the Most Dramatic Rescues of Our Time
ALL THE MEN IN THE SEA

"In the telling tale of a harrowing rescue of seemingly doomed mariners, Krieger celebrates working-class heroes facing the wrath of the sea and the unforeseen consequences of corporate greed."

—David Shaw, author of *The Sea Shall Embrace Them*

"A vivid, authentic picture of a great untold sea rescue. . . . Krieger shows us men battling for their lives in extreme conditions and seamen working with consummate skill and determination and ultimate courage to save them from the raging sea's fury. The injuries and loss of life in this true saga are shocking, but the dedication of man to save his fellow man should inspire all readers with a renewed faith in what human beings can bring to a desperate occasion."

—Peter Stanford, president emeritus, national Maritime Historical Society

"Meticulous, balanced, heartbreaking, and exciting, ALL THE MEN IN THE SEA details what happens when a floating village of oil pipeline workers meets a huge hurricane at sea. . . . [It] belongs on the bookshelf of anyone interested in contemporary rescues and disasters."

—Robert Frump, author of *Until the Seas Shall Free Them*

ALL THE MEN IN THE SEA

MICHAEL KRIEGER

POCKET **STAR** BOOKS
New York   London   Toronto   Sydney   Singapore

A Pocket Star Book published by
POCKET BOOKS, a division of Simon & Schuster, Inc.
1230 Avenue of the Americas, New York, NY 10020

Copyright © 2002 by Michael Krieger

Originally published in hardcover in 2002 by The Free Press

All rights reserved, including the right to reproduce
this book or portions thereof in any form whatsoever.
For information address The Free Press, 1230 Avenue
of the Americas, New York, NY 10020

ISBN: 0-7434-7091-5

First Pocket Books printing November 2003

10 9 8 7 6 5 4 3 2 1

POCKET STAR BOOKS and colophon are registered
trademarks of Simon & Schuster, Inc.

Cover design by Patrick Kang
Front cover photo by Hulton-Deutsch Collection/Corbis

Printed in the U.S.A.

For information regarding special discounts for bulk purchases,
please contact Simon & Schuster Special Sales at 1-800-456-6798
or business@simonandschuster.com.

To the men of the Captain John, *the* Seabulk North Carolina, *the* Ducker Tide, *and the* DLB-269, *who risked their lives so that others might live. Also this book is dedicated to the men who didn't return and to those who are still suffering.*

ACKNOWLEDGMENTS

First, I would like to thank all those people mentioned in the story who gave so freely of their time and without whose assistance this book would never have been written. Thank you to proofreaders Christopher Burr, Chief of the Tropical Analysis and Forecast Branch of the National Hurricane Center, National Oceanic and Atmospheric Administration (NOAA); to Hendrik Tolman, Visiting Scientist at NOAA's Environmental Modeling Center; to retired tug captain Hardy Schmidt, who used to tow barges between Seattle and Alaska; to Robert Lee Lloyd, retired diver; and to Thomas Dunlap, Oklahoma's finest wildcat oil driller.

Also, thanks to John Day, meteorologist; to translators and guides German Velasco Poo and German Velasco Cano; to translator Maricruz Erickson; to assistants Gale Greenberg and Sue Ann Fazio Zderic; to Carol Bee, my able editor and friend; and to my longtime supporter, my wife, Susan

Krieger. Finally, my appreciation to my agent, Jane Dystel, and to her associate Miriam Goderich; to editor Stephen Morrow at The Free Press, whose suggestions certainly improved this book; to Leslie Jones of Simon & Schuster; and to Fred Hills, also at The Free Press, who has been an inspiration for over twenty years, though he never knew it.

CONTENTS

AUTHOR'S NOTE

Since all vessels and aircraft mentioned used twenty-four-hour/military time, it is the standard used in the book. Conversion from civilian time is simple, as illustrated by the following examples.

One minute after midnight = 0001
8:30 A.M. = 0830
Noon = 1200
3 P.M. = 1500
11:59 P.M. = 2359

PROLOGUE

Luis Domingo de la Riva gazed up at the great Clyde as the crane rotated its boom above him, swinging it toward some sections of oil pipe to be moved. The young Mexican deckhand was still learning his way around, and the twenty-four-hour bustle of work on the 269 never ceased to amaze him. A group of American divers passed on their way to the saturation chamber. They were the elite, the high-paid crew who did the most difficult work of making the final connections in the undersea oil pipeline they were building. Most of the vessel's crew were Luis's fellow countrymen, except for the dive crew, the head man, Richard Lobb, and some other "technicos" who kept all the specialized equipment running and were in charge of the anchor operations. Luis had heard that the company was owned by a rich Mexican, but the boy had never seen him. Luis just did as he was told and tried to absorb as much as he could in hopes of advancing and making more money. He knew little about the offshore oil business, but he was learning rapidly.

Luis knew that most of the world's oil and gas

initially came from wells on good old solid ground. Beginning with the first wells drilled in the latter half of the nineteenth century, the deposits that could be most easily extracted were those first depleted. As more and more resources on land were drained and oil was discovered in shallow coastal waters, a new industry emerged. In the late 1940s the first offshore wells were drilled in shallow water and undersea pipelines were laid to bring the oil and gas ashore. Then, as more discoveries were made in deeper water, the technology was de-veloped to exploit them. Huge offshore drilling rigs were anchored in the seabed or sometimes floated on top of it. Pipelines, often hundreds of feet beneath the surface, first had to be prefabricated on specially equipped barges or ships and then lowered to the ocean bottom and, once there, somehow held in place.

Although some ships were used for this work, most vessels were derrick-equipped barges especially built to lay undersea pipelines and to construct and repair the drilling platforms. The name given these barges, at least in the United States, where the largest offshore construction companies were headquar-tered, was "derrick lay barge." They were unpowered and were towed by tugs and by anchor/supply vessels.

The 269, on which Luis Domingo worked, was a derrick lay barge. Built in Japan in 1967 for Brown and Root, then one of the largest offshore contractors in the world, *DLB-269* was 400 feet long by 100 feet wide and had a 19-foot draft. She carried stacks of oil pipe. Sections were laid end-to-end in an assembly line in a special "pipe alley," which ran from near the bow to a stern ramp that dropped into the sea. Two cranes onboard moved heavy materials, including pipe sections, which might be 40 feet long by 3 feet in diameter and weigh over two tons. The concrete-covered sections were welded together in the pipe alley, then checked with X-ray machines to make sure the welds were solid and there were no holes through which oil or gas might leak.

Derrick lay barges move along preset pipeline courses like floating spiders, pulled by retrieving cables to giant anchors, which are put down, picked up, and then reset by accompanying tugs and anchor tenders. As a barge moves, a pipeline drops off the stern, lowered diagonally from the end of a "stinger," which protrudes from the barge's transom. Once the pipeline is on the seabed, divers are lowered in a diving bell to make final undersea connections. Then a jet sled, lowered from and towed behind the barge, blasts a trench beneath the pipe using high-pressure water jets. The pipe drops into the trench and then is covered by sand or silt blown over it by the jet sled.

These operations require welders, inspectors,

PART I

Chapter One

0630 hours, Tuesday, October 10, 1995

THE LAST TWO divers down before Hurricane Roxanne hit were Lee Lloyd and Rob Whaley. They were working at 160 feet, making the final connections between two sections of a pipeline that would carry natural gas from an offshore oil and gas field in Bahia de Campeche, 60 miles off Mexico's Yucatan Peninsula.

Lee was in the hammock in the diving bell, relaxing and trying to keep an eye on his partner, Rob, who was attempting to line up two pipe sections so he could put the last bolts through the flanges and the gasket that sat between them, thus sealing the connection. This would then complete the work on that section of pipeline. One diving partner normally worked for four or five hours at a stretch, while the other relaxed in the bell only a few feet away and looked out for the safety of the man outside. Halfway through the eight- or ten-hour shift the two partners changed places.

In this part of the Gulf of Mexico there were few living hazards—sea urchins and the occasional moray eel—but most creatures stayed out of the divers' way. The exceptions were some members of the grouper family, which often weighed three or four hundred pounds and were equipped with formidable sets of teeth. Though a grouper could easily swallow a diver's arm in its cavernous jaws, it was almost always benign, a huge 6-foot-long puppy dog of the sea. It did, however, have one unfortunate trait. It was maddeningly curious. Divers tell stories of working on the bottom and suddenly having a creepy feeling that something was watching them. The shock of turning to see this monster 6 inches away staring into their facemask could almost blow a diver out of his weight belt. Divers say they often give the offending grouper a punch in the nose or simply push it away. Still, they never know for sure how the normally inoffensive grouper will respond, and the creature has been known to inflict painful bites.

The danger to the diver isn't groupers, however. It is working with heavy construction equipment and materials in a hostile environment where visibility is usually so poor that a blind diver might be better able to perform the tasks required and where the diver's precious life support consists of a few slender hoses and wires.

Rob Whaley was using a jet hose to excavate mud from under the end of a section of pipe. He aimed one side of the T-shaped nozzle under the pipe he wished to lower. Air from the barge, blasted through a hose at 250 psi, was a great excavator. However, Rob could only guess at how much silt he had been removing. They were working the night shift using battery-powered lights strapped on them, but even now, at dawn, there wasn't much light. To make matters worse, silt billowing through the water obscured what little might have been visible. Rob couldn't even see the pipe 2 feet in front of him, but had to work by feel, a situation common in underwater construction.

The 24-inch-diameter pipes Whaley was trying to align were far too heavy to move by hand. Besides, the two pieces of pipe he was trying to connect were each welded to section after section behind them. So, in effect, he was trying to move two pipelines. A lifting sling lowered by cable from one of the cranes on the 269's deck had cradled one of the two sections in an attempt to line up the pipes, but every movement of the barge made the flanges on the ends of each section jerk up and down. The 269 was not riding in heavy seas. Even so, the eight large anchors holding her in position could not prevent her from heaving over the swells that swept the barge. Trying to put drift pins in the bolt holes to temporarily align them until bolts could be fitted was far too dangerous when the pipe was held in a sling. Not only could Rob's fingers or hand be pinched between the sections, but a swell could suddenly jerk the sling enough to pop a ball valve in the line, which temporarily sealed it. The natural gas at high pressure inside, if suddenly released, could blow his diving helmet off. Or his umbilical might get entangled in or severed by the crane line. In either case he would be without both air and communication, fumbling in the dark with a dense cloud of silt obscuring everything around him. His umbilical, which fed from the diving bell, was also his only guide to get back to it. Without it he could easily be disoriented and lose his way.

The stories of divers trapped on the ocean floor were legion in the commercial diving world. Rob was well aware of the dangers, so he disconnected the sling and asked Tim Noble, the dive supervisor on duty on deck, to tell the crane operator to pull the sling up. Now he was trying to use the jet hose to drop the uppermost of the two pipe ends a few hundredths of an inch to allow him to jam in at least one of the foot-long tapered-steel drift pins. Rob, quiet and serious, depended for his safety on the instincts and experience he had developed in fifteen years as a commercial diver. He also knew he could count on Lee, his good-natured, lanky North Carolina dive partner, and on Tim, the savvy ex-Navy supervisor, listening to him on the intercom. Both Rob and Lee had been diving, first in the Navy and then in underwater construction, all their adult lives.

Lee, still in the bell, with his mask off, fed some slack air hose to Rob, who, judging from the moving cloud of silt that enveloped him, was working his way down the pipe section removing mud with the jet hose as he went. Lee couldn't see his partner but could hear him describing his movements over the intercom to Tim. The diver in the bell could hear both the working diver and the man above but could speak only to his partner. The bell was pressurized to their working depth, and this kept water from coming in above the hatch level and allowed the men inside to remove their masks—modern lightweight fiberglass helmets. The divers also wore neoprene suits with veins that distributed hot water, pumped from the barge, over their bodies. In this way they could work for hours in water temperatures that were often in the 40° range.

The 12-foot-high diving bell stood fairly upright

because the sandy bottom was nearly level where they were working and there were no coral heads. The bell itself was cylindrical, 7 feet across, and had a narrow hatch 3 feet up from the base plate. Around the outside were portholes and below them were strapped enough gas bottles filled with oxygen, nitrogen, and helium to supply two divers for a least twenty-four hours in case, because of some emergency, their supply from the barge was interrupted and they could not be pulled to the surface.

Lee was still feeding out hose when Tim gave them the word to shut down. They were going to be brought up for weather. A storm was coming. Rob fastened the jet hose to the down line hanging next to where he had been working and told Tim to have it hauled in. Then he joined Lee in the bell and together they dogged the hatch. Rob told Tim they were ready to go up.

With a slight jerk at the end of its long steel cable, the bell began its ascent. It would take about five minutes to reach the barge. As the remaining water was pumped from inside the bell, the 160-foot pressure level was maintained by pumping in more of the same oxygen-helium mixture the men were already breathing.

The diving bell Rob and Lee were riding in and *Derrick Lay Barge 269*, to which it was attached, belonged to a Mexican-American joint venture company, Corporacion de Construcciones de Campeche, S.A. (C.C.C.). J. Ray McDermott, the offshore construction branch of the huge American conglomerate McDermott International, owned 49 percent of C.C.C., and Grupo Consorcio de Fabricaciónes y Construcciones, S.A. (C.F.C.), owned by Felix Cantu Ayala, a wealthy Mexican industrialist, owned 51 percent. C.C.C. was under contract with Pemex, Mexico's national oil company, to build undersea pipelines connecting offshore oil drilling platforms in Bahia de Campeche, the large bay formed by the curve of Mexico's Gulf Coast as it swings east and then north along the Yucatan Peninsula.

In the 1960s extensive oil deposits had been discovered in the relatively shallow waters along the coast, and major offshore fields had been developed in four different areas. *DLB-269* was working in a field 60 miles north of Isla del Carmen, a 27-mile-long barrier island at the base of the Yucatan Peninsula. Ciudad del Carmen, the small city situated on the western end of the island, is an oil development center. Behind it stretches 50-mile-long Laguna de Términos, a shallow, almost totally enclosed saltwater bay. Although numerous small oil-supply craft normally anchor in this bay, C.C.C. considered it too shallow to accommodate the unwieldy

269 with its 19-foot draft, except in an emergency. So when the barge needed servicing it was towed to shipyards in Veracruz or Tuxpan, 260 or 350 miles to the west.

The bell broke the surface and continued its ascent until, with a jolt, it clanged up against a tubular steel framework extending over the side of the 269. Dive tenders, who handled the diving equipment, locked the bell onto the end of the saturation chamber, making sure there was an airtight seal. Then the whole apparatus slid on stainless steel rollers back onto the deck of the barge. Lee and Rob opened the bell port and stepped into the saturation chamber, a 7-foot-wide by 12-foot-long steel pipe made into an "apartment" that was shared by the six working divers when they were off duty. Living inside the "sat" chamber, which was pressurized to the depth at which the divers had been working and was supplied with the same gas mixture the men had been breathing in the bell and on the ocean floor, allowed them to avoid going through perhaps two days of decompression before they could set foot on deck. With no saturation chamber to keep them pressurized, they would need to spend two days decompressing for every day they worked at 160 feet. This way they could dive every day.

Usually the divers spent weeks at a time in their

pressurized barrel of a home. The sat chamber had double-deck, fold-up bunks hinged to the wall, a small table with four chairs, and at one end a sink and a toilet separated from the living area by a curtain. The divers showered in the diving bell using a hose. Food was sent in three times a day through an airlock. The sat chamber was not only the divers' home, it was their prison. While it was under pressure, the door was sealed shut. If, for some reason, the chamber lost pressure or the divers stepped out on deck, they would have perhaps five minutes before they died of an extreme case of the bends called explosive decompression. Within that five minutes nitrogen would overload their tissues and cause bubbles in their arteries. In humans the resulting embolisms produce either fatal heart attacks or strokes unless, somehow, they are immediately repressurized.

Lee and Rob joined the other divers in the chamber. "What's going on?" Rob asked. Usually another pair of divers would be ready to take the bell right back down, for, as they well knew, the entire expense of the whole barge operation and its 243 other workers, as well as the two tugs and their crews, rested squarely on the shoulders of the two working divers. So not a minute could be wasted. This time, however, no one was going down, at least not yet. Trouble was brewing.

As the first rays of sun glared over the horizon, Tim Noble came up the ladder from the radio room, where he had been meeting with Chuck Rountree, the diving superintendent; Roy Cline, the other diving supervisor; and Richard Lobb, the barge superintendent. Chuck headed the 269's twenty-man diving contingent. Tim and Roy were his assistants. Each of them ran diving operations during a twelve-hour shift. Lobb was the overall commander of the barge. Tim had just seen Danny Miller's weather printout of a new storm that appeared to be heading toward the 269. Danny, the ship's electrician, used his personal laptop to tie into INMARSAT, the International Maritime Satellite System. The weather map he had downloaded showed that the new storm had reached hurricane status and was banging Cozumel and the east side of the Yucatan with 80-mile-an-hour winds. Roxanne, the new hurricane, was centered a hundred miles east of Cozumel and had changed course. Now she was traveling west-northwest at about 5 miles an hour. If she stayed on her present course, she'd be passing the 269 in about four days, or much sooner if her speed increased. It was not out of the question that she might speed up at any time. In any case, it would not be long before they felt the brunt of her winds.

When Tim joined Roy, Chuck, and Richard in the radio room, they were studying a Wilkens printout that had just come in over the telex. Wilkens Weather Technologies is a Houston company that provides weather data to most of the offshore oil and gas industry operating in the Gulf of Mexico. Wilkens bulletins came in four times a day. An 1800 hours report the previous day had still shown Roxanne as a tropical storm heading northwest on the other side of the Yucatan. The latest, 0600, printout confirmed Danny Miller's INMARSAT report.

After looking at the two weather bulletins the four men agreed that they had to shut down and prepare for the hurricane. Orders were given to immediately start decompressing the divers in the saturation chamber. Also the barge's two assisting vessels, the *Captain John* and the *Seabulk North Carolina*, were called on VHF and told to help the 269 bring in her anchors and to get ready to take her under tow.

What became Hurricane Roxanne had first been recorded on October 7 as a tropical depression in the western Caribbean off the east coast of Nicaragua. As it headed northwest it briefly touched shore at the most easterly point of the border between Nicaragua and Honduras. Then it swung directly north, picking up wind speed and heading back out to sea. By noon on October 9, now a tropical storm with winds nearing 50 miles an hour, it began changing direction again, aiming toward the Yucatan.

At certain times of the year, early in the hurricane season (June and July) and late in the season (October and November), the northwest Caribbean seems to be a favored area for hurricane development. Warm currents running through the Yucatan Straits boost water temperatures, already in the upper seventies, to 79° or higher. This is the critical minimum water temperature to form and sustain a hurricane. (Some meteorologists set 81° as the minimum necessary water temperature.) At 79° or higher, enormous amounts of heat and moisture rise into the atmosphere, where they condense, producing rain and thunderstorms. When they come into contact with a tropical cell of low pressure, normally flowing from the east and usually originating off the west coast of Africa, it is like pouring gasoline on a small fire. Just such a tropical area of low pressure, tracked from the African coast on September 26, reached the western Caribbean on October 7 and interacted with the disturbed weather. Prior to this influence the broad low-pressure area then centered off the east coast of Nicaragua had generated winds of only 10 to 20 miles an hour.

If surface winds are traveling in the same direction as the low-pressure cell moving at a higher altitude, so that the heat and moisture rising from the ocean are not sheared away from the upper-level low but are able to flow up into it, feeding its power, all the ingredients then are in place to produce a hurricane.

The National Hurricane Center in Miami, which tracks, gathers information on, and provides warnings about hurricanes and other tropical storms, also names them. Since Roxanne was the seventeenth tropical storm to appear in the Atlantic / Caribbean / Gulf of Mexico in 1995, the hurricane center gave her a name starting with the letter R. (Names are assigned in al- phabetical order, but Q, U, X, and Z are omitted be- cause there aren't enough names beginning with those letters.)

Over the next two days Roxanne's winds steadily intensified, from a tropical depression on the seventh, with barometric readings of 1004 millibars and 35-mile-an-hour winds, to 989 mb and 60 mph winds on the ninth, to a full-fledged hurricane on the morn- ing of the tenth.

By 0600 on October 10 not only had the winds increased steeply but the barometric readings had plummeted, from 985 mb at midnight to 972 mb six hours later. Prior to the tenth, Roxanne, responding to a weak (low-pressure) trough over Florida and the eastern Gulf of Mexico, appeared to be threatening Cuba and the Caymans. However, the trough moved eastward, to be replaced by a band of high pressure. This pushed Roxanne northwest, then west toward the Yucatan. By midday, Roxanne was less than 400 miles away from the unwieldy barge and her two tugs.

While they are at work, the 269 and other undersea-pipeline-laying barges must be held rigidly in place, which is accomplished by spreading huge anchors around them. The 269 carried eight 30,000-pound stockless anchors, two on each corner of the vessel. These were positioned by one of the accompanying tugs, and the slack was then taken up by the barge's 100-ton-capacity winches. Now, with a hurricane bearing down on them, the process began in reverse. These maneuvers would require precise synchronization among all three vessels and their crews. Much like the members of a football or basketball team, the men had to work together to successfully complete the complex anchor raising.

Kevin Dumont and Steve Howell sat in the tower, a steel-and-glass structure that looked like an airport control tower and stood high above the starboard side of the main deck. In front of them were two radar repeaters and two monitors that displayed anchor positions and depths relative to the exact location of the barge. Using satellite positioning, the two anchor or tower operators could, by easing or tightening tension on a combination of cables leading to the eight anchors splayed around the 269, position the huge craft within a foot or two of any particular location on the sea floor. They now looked on, with Chuck Allday, one of the two anchor foremen standing behind them, as the 269's two tugs stood by to begin taking in the anchors.

Over VHF Kevin Dumont called the smaller of their attendant vessels. "*Captain John, Captain John,* Whiskey-Charlie-Yankee 5568, this is *DLB*-269. Come on in, Cap'n Robert."

After a pause and static came a casual reply: "This is *Captain John,* Whiskey-Charlie-Yankee 5568, back to *DLB*-269. Mornin', Kevin. Whatcha got for me? Over."

Robert Trosclair and Kevin Dumont had much in common. Both were of Cajun extraction, both came from the same small town in southwest Louisiana, and in years past the tug captain had worked with Kevin's father when the senior Dumont was himself a barge superintendent. Now Kevin passed instructions on to Trosclair concerning the first buoy to be picked up.

"Hey, Cap'n Robert," Kevin answered, "we're starting with port stern brest. Over to *Captain John.*"

"Roger, Roger, 269, I read you. *Captain John* over." With a swirl of foam the *Captain John* slid the length of the 269, keeping a hundred yards off her port side until the tug approached the first of the four large cylindrical buoys bobbing in the sea, fanned out from the rear of the barge. Trosclair backed the tug down on the buoy until two deckhands leaning over the transom snapped a shackle on a loop of cable, called a pendant, which went through an eye at the top of the buoy. Once Kevin knew that the tug had the buoy, he flipped an anchor toggle that released tension on the line to that anchor and called, "OK, Cap, you ready on that port stern brest? I'm slacked off on my anchor."

By this time the tug's crew had shackled the anchor's pendant line to their winch and had begun bringing it in until they had the anchor up against their transom. Trosclair was back on the radio. "The anchor's up, Kevin."

"OK, Cap, I'm gettin' up on ya." Kevin answered after he threw his winch in gear and began reeling in the anchor cable hanging between the barge and the anchor on the tug's transom. As soon as Trosclair felt the slack going out of the cable, he reversed the tug's engines and at slow astern angled for the port quarter of the barge. At a distance of 1,000 feet Trosclair asked Kevin to slow the speed at which he was bringing in cable. Then Trosclair edged the *Captain John* toward the fair-lead 30 feet forward of the barge's transom, where the anchor line fed into the winch.

Robert Trosclair was operating his tug from controls in the doghouse, the glassed-in cubicle overlooking the afterdeck. When the stern of the tug was about 100 feet from the barge, Trosclair was back on the radio. "I'm turnin' her loose, Kevin." Trosclair's deckhands released the anchor. The anchor's pendant line rolled freely off his drum. When the anchor was alongside the barge, Kevin locked his winch. Chuck Allday, now on deck near the stern, gave the order to the operator of the barge's big crane, who had been standing by, to go ahead and pick up. The huge Clyde rotated until the boom end was above the tug's transom. Then the operator dropped his hook, picked up the 2,000-pound buoy, and swung it over the barge. The buoy and its pendant line dropped slowly to the deck. The buoy lay next to the crane tub with its pendant cable falling on top of it. Then the crane laid the anchor on special chocks made to hold it.

By this time Steve Howell, working the bow anchors, had the *North Carolina* picking up the starboard bow brest. They continued until they had raised all but the last bow and stern anchors—which would be brought in after the tow had been established. Even then the last bow anchor would not be laid on deck but would hang from the fair-lead so it could be rapidly lowered in the event of some emergency.

The *Captain John*, a 110-foot tug built in 1984, was powered by three Detroit diesels. Together they produced nearly 4,000 horsepower and drove three 90-inch props in fixed Kort nozzles—big steel rings around each propeller that channel water through them, increasing thrust. She was a classic-looking seagoing tug except for the doghouse, which had been built behind the exhaust stack to provide a steering station overlooking her afterdeck. The other vessel, the *Seabulk North Carolina*, was a 190-foot anchor/oil-rig supply vessel with a 100-foot open deck aft where oil pipe could be carried. She also had large tanks below deck for fuel, drinking water, drilling mud, and other liquids, along with food and equipment storage areas so that she could supply either barges like the 269 or offshore drilling platforms. The *North Carolina* was built in 1979 and rebuilt in 1993. Her two EMD diesels produced 4,000 hp and drove two stern props and a thruster built into a transverse tunnel in her bow. She was also designed to be used as a tug, and because of her greater size she was somewhat more effective than the *Captain John*, so she was used as the primary tow. With preparations completed to take the towline, she began backing down in front of the barge.

Meanwhile, on deck two gangs of roustabouts, called *maniobristas*, had been working with the crane operators. One gang of six men and a foreman on the bow had been helping position the buoys on the chocks as they were brought aboard by the small Manitowoc crane, which crawled along the deck on its bulldozer-type tracks. Then they coiled the 1½-inch pendant cables next to each buoy. On the stern the other gang worked with the big crane's operator. Raising the anchors was an especially busy time for them.

One of the *maniobristas* stood apart from the group on the stern. He was new to the 269, had been onboard only two months. The newcomer, Luis Domingo de la Riva, was one of the youngest men on the barge. He had just turned nineteen. Standing by himself on the fringe of the group of roustabouts Luis kept his place as the least senior of the men around him. Many of his fellow deckhands considered him a green kid, hardly more than a child. Part of the problem was that he looked like a kid. Skinny and small, at 5 feet 5 inches and 120 pounds, he appeared more like a boy than a man. He ate continually but never gained a pound or grew an inch. To compensate for his size Luis Domingo had started to grow a mustache. Maybe it would make him look older. Unfortunately, it didn't grow big and bushy like some that other deckhands sported. It grew in so puny that it looked as though it belonged on his grandmother. However, he was told that it would fill out as he got older, so he left it. Luis tried to blend in. There were a few other young guys on the crew with whom he occasionally could pal around, but there wasn't a lot of time to do anything but work his twelve-hour shift, sleep, eat, and watch a movie. Sometimes he worked out in the exercise room, but mostly he was too tired at the end of his workday.

For the past few days Luis Domingo had been cleaning on deck, sometimes on his knees scrubbing with a wire brush. This was not anyone's favorite job, but he usually worked hard. The foremen knew who was doing the work and who was dogging it. If the bosses thought you were not working diligently, you would get a one-way boat ride ashore, and *adios!* If that happened, Luis's family would be extremely disappointed. Luis's mother's brother had gotten him the job through a friend, and the family expected him to send part of his monthly $300 earnings to help his mother, still living in a poor farming village 50 miles from the coast. After leaving school when he was fourteen, Luis had not been able to find work for nearly four years. It had been especially difficult at home because there had not been much money. This was his big chance and he was not going to blow it.

While Luis Domingo looked on, the foreman came up and diverted half of the group to help forward, securing the small crane's boom. As soon as they were under tow, the tracked Manitowoc rumbled down between four large steel eyes welded to the deck near the bow. It dropped its boom to the deck, facing aft horizontally. The *maniobristas* chained the crane in place and waited for the Clyde's boom to be lowered diagonally across the boom of the smaller crane. The huge Clyde sat on the stern. Looking like a main gun turret on an old battleship—minus the gun barrels—its 80-foot-long machinery house rotated on a 60-foot-diameter turret. The heliodeck, the helicopter-landing deck, was in front of the crane, though off-center on the starboard side so the Clyde's 260-foot boom could be lowered alongside. The track-riding sat chamber, with a gas and control shack perched on top and the diving bell attached on the starboard end, ran out from under the heliodeck so the diving bell could be lowered over the side, then tracked back under the heliodeck, where it was now positioned for bad weather. Forward and also on the starboard side was the tower. The eight sea buoys that the *maniobristas* had just secured rested in pairs on chocks along each side on the stern and two-thirds of the way up the bow.

Luis Domingo watched as the Clyde's operator, with a deft touch, slowly swung the long boom and gently laid it diagonally over the boom of the Manitowoc. Then Luis and three of his fellow deckhands lashed the two booms together. As Luis Domingo

Chapter Two

✦

BY EARLY AFTERNOON Tuesday, Superintendent Lobb and Joe Perot, C.C.C.'s operations chief and Lobb's boss back in Ciudad del Carmen—the closest port and city, 60 miles away—had made a fateful decision. It would determine the future of the 269, her two tugs, and all the men onboard the three vessels. Two other barges belonging to C.C.C. had also been working in the oil field. The *Sara Maria* was a smaller derrick barge used only to work on offshore oil platforms. During Hurricane Opal, which had hit the Gulf two weeks before Roxanne, the *Sara Maria* had dropped her big storm anchor and was still dragged more than 50 miles until she was nearly thrown onshore. When Roxanne came along, the barge's superintendent, Doug Hebert, demanded that she be towed into the sheltered bay at Carmen. The old lay barge *Mega Dos*, similar in size to the 269, was also towed in. Yet Richard Lobb and Joe Perot decided that the 269, which was working in the same general areas as the other barges, would ride out the hurricane under tow.

Richard Lobb was a big man, 6 feet 2 inches and muscular. Even in his middle fifties he was in reasonably good shape without having to exercise. Lobb had worked his way up on the oilfield barges, from lining up pipe sections for welding to foreman to superintendent, and had been in that position on the 269 for many years.

At any hour of the day or night, Lobb could be seen conferring with one of his foremen or supervisors or striding down the deck in a neatly pressed shirt and jeans to be present wherever or whenever an important operation was taking place. The 269's head man, a gravel-voiced good-old-boy from Port Arthur, Texas, was friendly, but he was all business. He made sure every job was done correctly. Lobb personally checked the barge's log, in which every major occurrence during each six-hour period was noted. And besides demanding careful work, he required personal neatness of every man onboard.

Mexican law dictates that every vessel registered in that country must have a Mexican captain in charge. The 269's regular captain was off duty and temporarily ashore. In his place was Acting Captain Miguel Alvarez Cantu. Several crew members reported, however, that Cantu was licensed only to operate a vessel no larger than 7,500 tons, and the 269 was over 8,000 gross tons. If his license was in fact limited to smaller vessels, Cantu was not legally qualified to captain her. In any case, according to many of the divers and barge crew, the Mexican captains were figureheads. On all important questions both captains deferred to Richard Lobb. They didn't spit without first getting his permission. The crew members agreed: on the 269 Richard Lobb was king.

The one person Lobb did defer to was Joe Perot. During the days ahead they would have frequent radio consultations. Everyone else took orders from Lobb, even the diving contingent, who theoretically were independent of his authority. If anyone disobeyed his orders, that person could be riding the next crew boat ashore, possibly out of a job. Sure, they could complain to the company, but probably to no avail.

Besides seeing that the work was done correctly, Lobb was to see that it was done on time. But the barge was weeks behind in her work schedule. And now that they had to discontinue operations to prepare for the hurricane, they would fall even further behind. Completing the work was vitally important to C.C.C. because it would bring to a close a $27 million contract with Pemex and thus the contractor would receive all the money the oil company owed it.

There was a major problem, however. The Pemex-C.C.C. contract called for the work to be completed August 23, 1995, 180 days from the time the job began. For every day past August 23 that the work was not completed, a penalty of 0.2 percent (1 percent for every five days) of the contract amount was to be deducted. On October 10, when the divers were brought up, the 269 was already seven weeks behind schedule. Delays due to acts of God (including storms) were deducted from the penalty amount but only if the storms were so severe that the Ciudad del Carmen port captain closed the port. The port had been closed for only a few days owing to the two preceding hurricanes, so already nearly $1.5 million in penalties were due to be deducted. If the 269 were towed to a safe port, nonreimbursable towing time would certainly exceed one and maybe two days— read an additional $54,000 to $108,000 in penalties. If, on the other hand, the 269 held position just east of the work site, only a few hours would be lost towing in each direction. It would later be argued that this was a mighty incentive for C.C.C. to keep the

269 in the oil patch. Lobb, however, would later dispute this charge.

Of course there were other considerations in dealing with the hurricane. The entrance to the sheltered bay at Carmen was shallow and the channel poorly marked. Then the bay itself was even more shallow. They could drag the 269 in, but they might have a major job towing her out again. There were two other ports, but they were farther away. The closest one was Dos Bocas, about 100 miles to the southwest, and the other, Coatzacoalcos, was more than 180 miles. So unless either Joe Perot or Richard Lobb had a change of heart, they would take on the storm under tow. No doubt the two men realized that there was always some risk in keeping the barge at sea, but it had survived countless storms in the past, so why shouldn't it now?

Throughout the barge, preparations were underway. In the galley the cooks were making what might be the last hot meal for the next few days. Below the living deck even more frantic activity was taking place, especially on the machinery deck. This, the lowest deck, running nearly the entire length and width of the 269, housed all the mechanical equipment that operated the various systems needed for the barge to do her work and to provide up to 250 men with good living conditions.

Forward on the machinery deck, engineer's assistants were securing everything that wasn't already lashed down in the various compartments containing generators, compressors, the desalination pumps and tanks (which produced the huge amount of fresh water needed every day), the air-conditioning and refrigeration equipment, and most of the vessel's other large operating machinery.

Aft of the machinery spaces, in an open area running the width of the bottom deck, two of the six stairwells led up to the accommodation deck and then topside. The large elevator also was located here. Pieces of machinery or bulky supplies were raised to or lowered from the main deck in it. At the aft end of the barge, machinists secured everything that wasn't already bolted to the deck in the two shops. Lathes and other steel-fabricating equipment filled one room, and woodworking equipment—saws, planers, and joiners—filled the other. The shops could build or repair almost anything the 269 might need. The object was to keep the barge out in the field as much as possible, rather than in a shipyard, where she would not be earning her keep. So all maintenance and repairs that did not require her to be hauled out of the water were accomplished onboard. Her crew could themselves repair almost anything that broke down. Spare parts were helicoptered in or were delivered by a crew or supply boat, along with any specialized technicians required. However, on a twenty-eight-year-old vessel, many of the repairs were simply patches upon patches. She was nearing the end of her useful life.

Just forward of the shops was the warehouse. In this cavernous space rows and rows of steel shelving extended up to the ceiling. On them sat thousands of replacement parts for nearly every piece of equipment on the barge. Spare equipment too large to fit on the shelves lay on the deck. Besides all the parts and extra equipment, the warehouse contained most of the tools required for repairing or operating anything onboard. If someone needed a spare part or a tool, that person (and only authorized personnel or managers were allowed to check out tools or parts) would first go to the office, one of the few air-conditioned spaces on the usually sweltering machinery deck.

The office was the private domain of the two genial warehouse managers. Both were among the older members of the crew and both were respected by almost everyone. Gustavo Zaldivar, a calm, balding, bespectacled forty-eight-year-old, was married, with two grown sons. He had been on the 269 only five months but had worked in the offshore oil industry all his adult life. Gustavo worked the night shift.

His counterpart, "El Padre," Juan Adolfo Gomez Cruz, was a deeply religious man whose friendly smile radiated good feeling wherever he went. "*Buenos dias*, Padre," people would call out to him as he passed. He too called people by that name so there is speculation that this practice was the basis for his nickname. Others said no, he got his nickname because he was so religious. In days to come when the 269 was in trouble, El Padre laboriously wrote out prayers for the crew and posted them outside the mess hall. El Padre was forty-six, had worked on the 269 for eighteen years, and was part of the original crew that had brought her down from the United States. He had two little boys, six and three, and a wife, Isabel. He would never see them again.

Both of the head storekeepers (their official title) kept the vast warehouse spaces immaculate and in perfect order. Now El Padre and his assistants were making sure that the cage doors that fronted all the parts bins and shelves were securely fastened and that every large item was lashed to the deck. All over the 269 similar activities were taking place as the crew tried to prepare their small floating town for what was to come.

Since 1300 on Tuesday, the barge had been under tow. The *North Carolina* and the *Captain John* were now steering 335° north-northwest, having changed course once they left the oil field. With bows into wind and seas, their speed of 3 knots, they hoped, would allow them and the 269 to roughly maintain their present position relative to the oil fields to the west and the shallows to the east and south, without putting undue strain on the towing cables. However, this became more difficult as they plodded on into higher seas and stronger head winds. With each hour, both seemed to increase as the storm descended on the three vessels.

The following day, Wednesday, October 11, the two dive supervisors and Chuck Rountree met with Richard Lobb. Tim Noble was angry. "You know, what the hell are we doing?" he said to the others. "We've got the guys [divers] out and we are decompressing them, but we're just taking our time. We should be accelerating their decompression." Lobb wondered if they had enough information on what the hurricane would do when and if it got back out to sea after crossing the Yucatan Peninsula. "Well, typically they [hurricanes] gain strength when they leave land and get back over water," Rountree replied. And with Roxanne closing in on them, they were already on the verge of receiving hurricane-force winds.

Since they were approximately 60 miles from shore, one possibility, if the situation got desperate, was just to beach the 269, but Lobb's next comment showed the problems with that choice. "You know, it's an old barge," he told them. "It could break up. If it gets on the beach, it *will* break up." Also, much of the shoreline to the east shoaled out a number of miles, and the 269 might never even reach the beach. They agreed that they needed emergency decompression for the divers and they needed it immediately. But the question was, How fast could you decompress them without the emergency decompression itself killing or injuring them?

Mike Ambrose had just returned from lunch to his temporary office in Morgan City, Louisiana, when he received the call. Mike, a former Navy SEAL and a diver for twenty-five years, was the worldwide operations manager of the diving division of Offshore Pipelines Incorporated. Offshore had been the 49 percent owner of the 269 in the C.C.C. partnership but had recently been acquired by J. Ray McDermott. Possibly the largest offshore contractor even before its acquisition of Offshore Pipelines, McDermott built offshore oil platforms and pipelines all over the world but specialized in Gulf of Mexico work. In the early 1950s it had installed the first all-concrete oil platform and the first platform in more than 100 feet of water. In 1956 it developed an extensive shipyard in Morgan City solely for the construction of offshore structures. In 1966 it had acquired a diving company, and since its takeover of Offshore, McDermott not only was a partner in the 269 but also was responsible for supplying the divers and dive support personnel for the 269's work.

Because of the McDermott/Offshore merger, Ambrose was temporarily without a job title, so he was filling in for McDermott's domestic operations manager, who was on vacation. In the rambling office complex that housed the headquarters of McDermott Underseas Services, the conglomerate's diving group, Ambrose listened to a worried Chuck Rountree over single-sideband radio. "We are in 14- to 16-foot seas, still on a heading of 335°," Rountree told him. Even over the radio's static Ambrose could hear the concern in the other man's voice as he continued, "But we're making minimal headway now, because of Roxanne. We've got an ETA for it to pass over us sometime between 1900 and 2300 tonight. And we've still got six divers in sat under standard navy decompression." Rountree went on to request that they start emergency decompression for the divers. No one wanted them to be trapped in the saturation chamber if the full force of a hurricane hit the barge.

"Immediately," Ambrose told Rountree, "eliminate the hold times you've been using [on the divers] and increase oxygen pressure in the chamber from 0.6 to 0.7—and increase decompression to 3 feet a minute." Then he told Rountree that he would get back to him as soon as he could get more information on further emergency decompression steps they should take.

As soon as he finished with Rountree, Ambrose called in the chief diving safety officer for Offshore, James J. Riddle, with whom he had worked closely in the past, and also McDermott's diving safety officer, Pete Patrasic. Together they pored over the emergency decompression tables and procedures that had been established by McDermott. However, those emergency procedures had never been used in the nine years since they had been initiated. While they had been carefully prepared, they were untested. In fact, according to Ambrose, the three men knew of no case anywhere in the world where those emergency procedures had been used. They might kill or totally disable the very men they were trying to help. Six lives were at stake and everyone was concerned about whether they could save them.

With hurricane-force winds expected to be over the barge in as little as six hours, time was not on the side of the divers. If the 269 sank with them still not fully decompressed, they would either drown, going down with the barge, or leave their sealed chamber and die of the bends, one of the more painful ways by which a human can exit this world.

Decompression sickness is a disease of our times. Almost unknown until men started working in deep mines and building underwater tunnels in the last century, it was named "the bends" because it often produces pain in the abdomen and joints that is so severe it will cause the victim to double over in agony. As a diver descends into the water (or someone goes deep underground), pressure greatly increases on the body, on air in the lungs, and on the air's main components, nitrogen and oxygen, which are dissolved in the bloodstream. The greatest problem is with the inert gas, nitrogen. When a diver or worker gradually ascends to the surface, the nitrogen can naturally leave the body slowly, as gas, through the lungs, which is why decompression takes so long. If the person returns too quickly to the surface, he is likely to have nitrogen trapped in the fatty tissues and in the lungs.

The trapped nitrogen forms bubbles in the bloodstream and the bubbles flow with the blood to various parts of the body. In the joints and in the stomach the bubbles expand, causing enormous pain. In blood vessels running through the bones there is no place for the bubbles to expand. Consequently they can block the thousands of small veins that run through the bones, especially in the long bones like the femur and the tibia. The result is a permanent

breakdown of the bones known as dysbaric osteo-
necrosis. In the 1958 building of the Clyde Tunnel
in Scotland nearly 20 percent of the workers experienced this disease, as did almost 35 percent of the
workers building a sewer tunnel in Milwaukee in
1969. Paralysis of the lower body and spinal cord injury are other results of decompression sickness, but
the worst scenarios, almost always resulting in death,
are embolisms, or blockages, in either the heart or the
brain. These embolisms, as mentioned earlier, are the
main causes of death in cases of explosive decompression.

So why, if inert gases like nitrogen or helium can
cause the bends, do not divers just breathe pure oxygen? Unfortunately, too great a concentration of oxygen in the body is just as toxic as the other gases.
Most people don't realize it, but we here on the
Earth's surface breathe far more nitrogen than
oxygen. Air at sea level is 79 percent nitrogen and
21 percent oxygen, with just traces of other gases and
organic matter. Lung damage may result from breathing a 60 percent or higher concentration of oxygen for
more than six hours. At greater concentrations the
nervous system is affected. Divers breathing too great
a concentration of oxygen can also experience con-
vulsions and seizures, both resulting in death.

Understanding only too well how little time

they had to help the divers, Ambrose and his assistants set out to verify whether the old emergency decompression procedures were still valid. Dr. Russ Peterson, a noted hyperbaric physician in Houston who had developed the procedures, was the first to be called, but he was out of town. His wife said she would try to track him down. Next, they called Dr. Gordon Daugherty, of Austin, Texas, the company's dive physician. Daugherty asked Ambrose to immediately fax him the tables and procedures. Daugherty then faxed them to Bill Hamilton, another hyperbaric-table expert. By that time Russ Peterson had called back. Together the three experts and the three diving officers came up with a plan that they hoped would run the fine line between getting the divers decompressed before the hurricane hit and giving them the bends. But no one knew for sure if it would work.

At 1445 that afternoon, only two hours after he had been alerted, Ambrose called Ed Burgueno, McDermott Undersea Services' representative at Ciudad del Carmen. He gave Burgueno the following instructions for him to relay to the 269 by single-sideband radio: "At 1530 hours, if you choose to commence emergency decompression, increase the elevation pressure rate to five feet per hour. Change and start the divers breathing 50/50 nitrox [nitrogen and oxygen] through BIB masks* at twenty minutes on / five minutes off cycles. At thirty-three feet switch to pure oxygen and continue the twenty minutes on / five minutes off cycles on BIB's. At ten feet depth commence a 110-minute hold (this will be the Diving Supt.'s call as to the conditions, and the threat of disaster that may exist at that time). If the vessel is in imminent danger at this time the divers should be brought to the surface. After completion of the 110-minute hold, slowly bring the divers to the surface. After surfacing, divers should remain in the vicinity of the recompression facilities and breath pure oxygen a minimum of ten minutes out of every thirty for the next six hours. This authorization is not a directive to implement this procedure but rather authority to do so should the on-site Diving Superintendent decide to do so."

Ambrose later explained the reasoning behind the procedure. "These efforts were to have the divers off gas as fast as possible by placing oxygen in their systems. Then after switching to air it was hoped that

---

*A B.I.B. (built-in breathing system) mask allows a different gas to be given to divers than what already exists in the chamber. Each diver inside the chamber wears a breathing mask connected by a supply hose to gas supplies outside the chamber. Each diver's mask also contains a regulator in an exhalation hose, also led outside the chamber. The regulator prevents the exhalation hose from taking the incoming gases the diver needs to breathe.

the helium would be purged from their bodies and that it would be replaced by nitrogen, but in a dilute form similar to what they would experience at sea level, out of the chamber."

Still, the ultimate decision whether to go to emergency decompression was left to the diving superintendent on the 269, Chuck Rountree, and to the divers themselves. Rountree quickly consulted with the six divers in the chamber as well as with his two diving supervisors and Richard Lobb. They all agreed they ought to go ahead. At 1515 Chuck called Ambrose back and told him, "OK, we're initiating it."

Even though the eye of Hurricane Roxanne was still to the southeast, and still on the eastern side of the Yucatan Peninsula, by 1800 Tuesday it had turned into a Category III hurricane, with winds approaching 115 mph. The barometer had fallen to 958 millibars, down from 972 in the past twelve hours. Like all hurricanes in the Northern Hemisphere, Roxanne whirled counterclockwise, so the wind and waves already driving into the 269 and her two tugs were coming from the northwest, not the southeast. As the wind began to howl and the seas grew, the 269, in spite of the cables securing her to the two tow vessels, started to heave vertically on each wave and to plunge into each succeeding trough. The tow cables would fall slack in the troughs, and then, as the barge rode up on a crest, they would spring out of the sea, the tremendous weight of the barge drawing them tight, to the breaking point, like great steel bow-strings. Waves broke over the three vessels, hitting them with explosions of water that cascaded along their decks, then gushed back into the sea. Rain pelted them in blinding torrents. The rapidly moving wiper blades on the bridge windows of the tug and supply boat seemed like useless appendages, and visibility was reduced to less than half a mile.

Early Tuesday morning when Rob Whaley and Lee Lloyd had finished their shift and rejoined the four other divers in the saturation chamber, they had been told that because of the storm on the other side of the Yucatan they would all start decompressing. Their mood was stoic. They had all been through storms at sea, including riding some out in saturation. So this was nothing new, not even particularly worrisome. But when Chuck Rountree, their diving superintendent, came down Wednesday afternoon to talk to them in person, speaking through the intercom outside the chamber, his first words were "I want to talk to everybody." That meant that anybody asleep had to wake up. Seldom was an announcement so important that divers working on a different shift and presently sleeping had to be awakened. Chuck's first sentence was enough to catch their attention.

Lee Lloyd explained it: "You don't hear that too often. If something's really screwed up or if there's something bad happening and your diving superintendent says that, everybody knows it is serious from the get-go."

"I've been talking to the beach," Chuck continued, "and I've had Mike Ambrose talking to the doctors in Houston. They are working out a schedule to bring you guys up earlier. We are thinking of escalating your decompression to get you guys out of there because of the hurricane coming and because we don't feel real good about the seaworthiness of this vessel. I'm talking to people right now, and we're trying to figure out what we're gonna do and I just wanted to let you guys know."

After Chuck finished, the six divers sat and looked at each other. Rob Whaley said, "Well, if he's concerned about it, Chuck's been around the block . . ."

Rountree was highly trusted by the men. Lee Lloyd said, "Everybody in that chamber knew that Chuck would do anything in his power to keep us safe. The same went for Tim Noble and for Roy Cline. Those guys were the kind, you know, that if somebody told them to do something that they thought might be detrimental to our safety, they would have punched them right in the face."

All three men had been Navy divers and then had gone into commercial diving, where they had worked at sea for decades all over the world. Tim was serious and thoughtful—and dependable. Roy was a boisterous Texan, a jokester, except when it came to work and the safety of his men. Then his personality changed, and his intelligence and knowledge took over. Chuck, the boss, was boyish and friendly. He knew his business backward and forward, and his every waking thought was addressed to the work at hand and his divers' safety.

The divers in the chamber normally would have been talking about work or some fishing trip or telling a funny story concerning a wife or girlfriend. Now they were silent. Of the six, two were younger. Phil Richard had been in commercial diving only a couple of years but was considered an up-and-comer. Clay Horschel was also a good younger diver. Lenn Cobb, in his early forties, had been diving commercially for twenty years and was highly regarded by the younger men. Rob Whaley, a former Marine, also had plenty of experience. So did another ex-Marine, special forces recon expert Rob Boettger. One of the diving leaders was Lee Lloyd. In his late thirties, Lee was tall and soft-spoken. From North Carolina originally, he had been living in southwestern Louisiana for a number of years because that's where the diving jobs were. Lee had always wanted to be a diver. He, Rob Boettger, and Lenn had worked all over the Gulf as well as in the North Sea, where bad weather was a way of life. So they were not impressed by the storm. That is, not at first.

Lee remembered the sequence clearly. "Anytime you're on a vessel and you're at sea and there's a hurricane coming, well, you prepare for the worst, but you never really think that your vessel's going to sink—unless you know something structurally or mechanically or physically is wrong. So you figure things might get rough, things might get knocked around but the vessel's gonna float. But anyway, when they told us, 'Hurricane's coming, we're going to start decompression,' OK, big deal. Well then, next thing you know, well, the hurricane looks like it's coming this way. You know, 'There's a hurricane coming, we're going to start decompression.' No big deal, it's happened a thousand times. Weather's coming, you're gonna start your guys up; nine times out of ten you never even get out [of decompression].

"Anyway," Lee continued, "then the next thing they tell us, our superintendent, Chuck Rountree, said, 'It's coming and it looks, on the track it's on, like it's gonna come right over us.' And he was getting kind of nervous. And, you know, we didn't feel good about it and weather's starting to pick up and you're in the chamber and you know it's getting rough. You can look out the portholes and you can see them starting to tie shit down and close the doors and rigging for rough weather—but still, it's happened before and it's nothing new. And everybody in there with the exception of a couple of divers were old. I say old—were fairly seasoned hands, they'd been around. So it wasn't 'Oh shit, hurricane's coming.' We all just kind of took it as not anything that serious—at least not until they decided on emergency decompression."

When at 1500 hours Chuck and Roy came back on the intercom and spelled out the emergency procedures the doctors had recommended, Chuck asked the divers if they wanted to undergo the emergency decompression. All said yes. As the divers began the procedures their calm exteriors didn't change, but they were acutely attuned to the buildup of seas and wind. More and more they felt the effects of the storm as the barge continued to rise and fall over the waves. The slack in the cables as one or both of the smaller vessels rode up the crest of a swell would suddenly go taut again, and those onboard would be jerked, sometimes off their feet if they weren't prepared. The odd piece of equipment that had not been secured hit the deck with a crash or went rolling across it. And the groans from the old 269, her thousands of joints flexing, gave signs of the stresses she was starting to undergo.

There was also an occurrence that weighed on the minds of all the divers and their handlers. It was not ancient history. It had happened only four years before. A sister barge to the 269, McDermott's *Derrick Barge 29*, with 195 men aboard, had been hit by a typhoon in the South China Sea. She too was under tow, running at a few meager knots, trying to escape the wrath of the storm. She too had divers, four of them, undergoing decompression in her sealed saturation chamber.

At daybreak on August 15, 1991, huge waves propelled by Typhoon Fred's 80-mile-an-hour winds broke loose a pair of 10-ton steel anchor buoys that been lashed on the 29's deck. Rolling across the open deck, they smashed, and smashed again, against the hatch cover of the vessel's water-desalination plant. Before anyone could do anything, the hatch cover was gone. Thousands, then tens of thousands of gallons of seawater poured through the hatch. Crew members tried to isolate the desalination space but they were too late. Too much water had already gotten in and they couldn't shut the steel doors leading to the adjoining spaces to contain it. The barge's pumps immediately went into action but they couldn't keep up with the seawater pouring in as wave after wave swept across the deck of *DB-29*. Another leak had started in the bow where a loose anchor dangling over the side had knocked a hole in the hull. The 29 was under tow by a 9,500-horsepower seagoing tug, far more powerful than either tug pulling *DLB-269*. So the weak link was not the 29's tug. It was her tow cable. The tremendous stresses created by towing a barge through hurricane seas while she was taking on hundreds of thousands of gallons of seawater snapped the towline. Immediately the 29 went broadside to the waves pounding her. And then she began to roll, slowly capsizing, slowly turning upside down.

Already at the sound of the alarm, the crew had donned life jackets and had congregated at their life stations. Only a few key men remained below at their posts—and of course the four divers trapped in the saturation chamber. The divers had been put on emergency decompression as soon as the broken hatch was discovered. But it had all happened so quickly that emergency decompression was useless. It would take fifteen hours, even at the accelerated decompression rate, for them to reach a level safe enough to exit the chamber without getting the bends.

As the 29 began to turn turtle, all the men went into the ocean, all but the four trapped divers and Billy Young, who was the barge superintendent, and three radio operators who never made it out. The alarm had gone out early in the emergency and fortunately the 29 was close to the major port of Hong Kong. Dozens of ships descended on the 29, still riding upside down on the surface. Most of the crew were rescued from the sea or from the 29's life rafts. Twenty-two men perished, including the four divers.

Evidently the divers, knowing that without power their saturation chamber would lose pressure, had thought it would be preferable to take their chances with the bends and maybe get help on the surface rather than simply to drown as the 29 sank deeper and deeper into the sea. It seems that in a last desperate act to try to save themselves, they slightly opened the large steel door sealing one end of their now depressurized chamber to gradually allow water to fill it. Then they floated to the surface. Three of them were later found, their bodies drifting on the ocean, dead of the bends. The body of the fourth diver was never found.

Many offshore dive vessels carry, as part of their sat chambers, detachable self-contained and self-propelled pressurized lifeboats, especially designed to save the lives of divers in saturation. However, such lifeboats are not required equipment in the United States or in most of the world. *DB-29* did not carry them, and neither did *DLB-269*.

The *269*'s divers were acutely aware of each

passing hour and their silent race to finish decompression before the full fury of the hurricane hit. In their cramped barrel they made extra efforts to stay in their own small spaces, perhaps to flop with a paperback in their bunks, so as not to infringe on the privacy of their fellows. Rob Whaley, Rob Boettger, and Clay Horschel were quiet by nature even at the best of times. Now they sank even further into themselves. The two Robs took everything in stride, and they were also tough emotionally and mentally. Normally they wouldn't hurt a flea, but you didn't want to mess with them. Clay was just as tenacious and disciplined, maybe more so. Lee's wife, Renee, called him "Deprivation Man" because even though he earned more than $80,000 a year, he preferred to live in a tent, even through snowy upstate New York winters. Clay always pushed himself physically to see how far he could go. Sometimes during his daily runs while onshore, he ran until he passed out.

The other three divers were different. Lee was easygoing, with a friendly chuckle and a love of humor. He was also intelligent and very knowledgeable about his field. Phil Richard, the handsome young diver, also loved to laugh and to party and have a good time. He was small, and maybe his modest stature gave him the impetus to excel at his work, in fact at everything he did. Phil and all the other divers liked Lenn Cobb. Everyone did. Lenn was a friendly country boy from Alabama who loved to fish and hunt and tell stories. He never got upset or even raised his voice.

But now Lenn's stories and Phil's joking and Lee's laughter had evaporated. The six divers read paperbacks or played chess or solitaire or were lost in their thoughts, wondering if they would ever again see their families and loved ones. The minutes and hours seemed to drag as they never had before.

Tim Noble had begun supervising the divers' emergency decompression. Then at noon, when his shift was over, Roy Cline came on and continued watching the divers through the observation port and communicating with them over the intercom. Roy made sure the divers were as comfortable as possible. The galley was no longer serving hot food, but the divers ordered the kinds of sandwiches they wanted and these were sent in through the airlock.

When Roy came on duty, so did Ron Rozmary-noski, the life support technician, who, from the control shack above the chamber, monitored all the divers' changing gas and pressure settings. Rozy also told them when and for how long to put on their special breathing masks. The divers had great confidence in both Rozy and Bob Wheeler, his counterpart, and the two technicians knew how crucial they were to the divers' well-being. One wrong gas setting could kill all of them. Often Roy or Chuck Rountree double-checked to make sure the stages of the decompression were progressing exactly as the doctors and Mike Ambrose had dictated. The life-support techs and the supervisors also thought that time seemed to drag interminably that day.

Unless you have experienced a hurricane, it is almost impossible to imagine the magnitude of the forces it thrusts upon those in its path. A hurricane produces a massive release of atmospheric potential energy. The storm's energy, released in its high winds and precipitation, in one day may average 300 to 400 billion kilowatt hours. This is more energy than that produced by all the hydroelectric dams in the United States in an entire year—or enough to provide electricity for 30 million residences. Such was the power of Roxanne. By 1500 Wednesday afternoon, now traveling west at 10 miles an hour, the hurricane was cutting a swath of destruction two hundred miles wide as she crossed the center of the Yucatan Peninsula. Twenty thousand tourists and residents had been evacuated from the Caribbean island of Cozumel and the resort areas of Cancún and Mérida ahead of her 110-mile-an-hour winds. Pemex closed its largest production facility at Campeche and evacuated its workers—just in time, too, because soon nearly all the major highways were impassably under water.

As Roxanne continued across the Yucatan her winds dropped but not the torrential downpours that accompanied her. Farmland that had already been flooded by Hurricane Opal now was totally inundated. Eighty percent of the corn and rice crops would be ruined. More than 1,600 cattle would drown and entire populations of many villages would be homeless. The poorest *campesinos*, whose houses were mostly of clay or old cardboard cartons, of course were hit the hardest. Their homes were gone along with their meager crops. Even if there had been sufficient relief supplies, there was no way to get them to those who so sorely needed them.

As the hurricane bore down on the 269, heavier winds gusted to more than 75 miles an hour, from the northwest. The seas, too, had increased, running between 18 and 20 feet and continuing to slam into the two tugs and the barge. So far the tugs had been able to hold the 269 into them. There was no question of attempting to flee. Their only two aims were to prevent the 269 from going broadside to the seas and to put as little stress as possible on the towing cables. Then, at 1620 Wednesday afternoon, one of the two cables parted.

There was no rifle-shot crack as the tow cable

broke, no violent sound to give testimony to the parting line. Just one moment it was there and the *Captain John* was straining to hold the 269, and the next moment the cable was gone and the tug was sailing free of her tow.

Immediately Robert Trosclair, the master of the *Captain John*, swung the tug in a broad arc to port to make sure she stayed clear of the *North Carolina* and her cable 200 yards on her starboard beam, as well as to move out of the path of the 269. Then he called the *North Carolina* on VHF.

"Echo-Kilo-Oscar 4895, *Carolina*, *Carolina*, this is *Captain John*, Whiskey-Charley-Yankee 5568. Richard—we just lost our cable. Over."

Richard Cassel, master of the *North Carolina*, responded immediately, "*Captain John*, Whiskey-Charley-Yankee 5568, this is *North Carolina*, Echo-Kilo-Oscar 4895. You lost your wire, yeah? How long you think before you back on? *Carolina*, over."

"Yeah, *Carolina*, we lost her. I think she broke near the drum. Lorenzo is down there now. We'll try to get a quick splice on her and get back on soonest we can. Over."

A relaxed response followed: "OK, *Captain John*. Let us know when you expect to be back on. This is *North Carolina*, Echo-Kilo-Oscar 4895, clear."

Then Trosclair called the 269. They were well

aware of the break. In fact they were already winch-
ing in the 1,800 feet of cable that was in the sea
curling over the 269's bow. They would put a splice in
their end and wait for the *Captain John* to come
alongside.

Lorenzo Wilson, the tug's Nicaraguan first
mate, and the three deckhands had winched the
cable remnant on deck. It had parted only a few
hundred feet from the tug's transom, so that task
was easily accomplished. They waited for Trosclair
to swing the bow back around into the seas to give
them a little protection from the waves, then set to
work. The afterdeck of a tug has little freeboard.
Usually it is only 4 or 5 feet above sea level. On the
Captain John the men were only a couple of feet
above the troughs and 10 or 12 feet below the
crests, which broke when they hit the tug, sending
torrents of water flooding across the deck on which
the men were working.

As the *Captain John* slid down a trough in front
of a big wave, the four men darted behind the large
winch-cable drums and turned to watch. The deck
suddenly foamed with three feet of white water. In a
moment the deck was clear and they were out again.
One man held the end of the 2½-inch-thick cable
while Lorenzo and another deckhand separated the
steel cable strands—not too difficult, since the

strands had partially unraveled as the cable broke. The men knew that with all the strain now taken by just one cable, that remaining cable was under extreme stress. If it broke, the barge would immediately go broadside to the seas. And if that happened the 269 would roll over, trapping the men below deck and signing the death warrants of the six divers in the sat chamber. Through their portholes the divers had seen the *Captain John* swing off to one side of the barge and they knew what it meant.

On the *North Carolina* Richard Cassel played his throttles, carefully easing them a bit as his boat rolled down into a trough, then gently increasing power going up a crest so as to put not an ounce more pressure than necessary on the remaining tow cable to hold the 269's bow into the sea.

The men working on the afterdeck of the *Captain John* ran behind the cable drum twice more to escape breaking waves. They wrapped the strands back around the cable head to form an eye, then twisted the strands back around each other. After another dash behind the drum they bolted two huge clamps around the two parts of the cable forming the base of the eye and tightened the bolts. Lorenzo yelled to the captain over his hand-held VHF that they were ready. The men waited by the engine room companionway while Trosclair powered the *Captain*

John out in front of the 269's bow. Next would come the most critical and dangerous maneuver.

Still going slow astern, Trosclair tried to time his speed in reverse to bring the transom of the tug just in front of the heaving bow of the barge at the same time as a large wave lifted the tug's afterdeck even with or above the weather deck of the 269. Normally the barge's deck would be 8 feet above the *Captain John*'s, but now it was sometimes 30 feet above it as the tug fell into a trough. The barge, still held under tension by the *North Carolina*, did not ride up over the waves or sink under them nearly as much as the tug that cowered before her.

As a large wave brought the tug's stern up above the bow of the 269, Lorenzo dashed out carrying a heaving line and with a broad sweeping motion flung a monkey's fist, a weighted ball of line with a dozen coils, toward the 269's deck. The wave quickly rolled past them, however, and by the time the heaving line went snaking out toward the barge, the *Captain John* had already fallen into the next trough. Instead of landing on the 269's deck, the line splashed into the sea.

Trosclair already had the *Captain John* in gear and quickly goosed the throttle to keep the tug from getting swept under the barge. Once he had a hundred feet separating the two vessels, he started again slowly backing the tug down toward the barge. Twice more he repeated the procedure and twice more Lorenzo heaved his line. Each time the line either fell harmlessly into the sea or bounced off the 269's bow, and each time Trosclair had to gun the tug away from what in just seconds would have been a fatal collision for the men on the tug's afterdeck.

Finally, on the fourth try, the heaving line went arching over the 269's deck. Crewmen immediately grabbed it and made it fast to a 2-inch-thick nylon hawser. This was winched aboard the *Captain John*. Attached was the other severed cable end, also formed into a new eye. The two eyes were bolted through the ends of a spare nylon snatch line, used to absorb stress on the tow cable, and at 1715, only fifty-five minutes after the cable had parted, the new tow cable was secure and the *Captain John* was back at her towing station.

The full fury of Roxanne blew upon them shortly after the towline had been reconnected. Eighty-mile-an-hour winds hurled 20-foot waves against them, but still the tow cables held. Through the night Robert Trosclair and Richard Cassel battled, each at the helm of his tug, trying to prevent further towline breakage. Backing off their throttles as their individual boats slid down troughs and bumping power back up again to keep them going up crests, they did as much as they could to keep the towlines from receiving sudden strains that might snap them.

At 0130 on Thursday, the six divers heaved sighs of relief as the saturation chamber door was undogged and they climbed the ladder to the dive office. Immediately, the barge doctor gave them the first of four neurological exams. The exam was sort of an expanded state trooper's drunk test to ensure that the divers had normal neurological function and that there was feeling in all parts of the body and no symptoms of decompression sickness. Eyes were checked with a flashlight for slow or retracted eye movement. A little wheel with prongs was run up and down limbs and torsos and a litany of questions was asked relating to possible symptoms of the bends. The neuro and a normal post-saturation-dive physical, checking heartbeat, blood pressure, and general well-being, were completed quickly. All the divers seemed fine. They each took their mask and portable oxygen tank with them, but they were told to stay near the sat chamber. They were to breathe pure oxygen for ten minutes out of every thirty for the next six hours. And none of them would be allowed to sleep until 1300 that afternoon. If you go to sleep and you are bent, you might not know it until you wake up, say eight hours later, and by that time you might have severe problems. This would be a long sleepless period,

tug, where they proceeded to rebuild the board and to repair the broken towline. The *North Carolina*, meanwhile, had slacked off her towline and just stood by to make sure that the 269 did not drag anchor.

Aside from the broken deck gear on the tug, the news that Friday morning was entirely good. Roxanne now was heading north-northwest toward Brownsville on the Mexico-Texas border. Even more important, the wind speed had continued to drop, to just over 50 miles an hour near the storm's center. By noon most of the men on the 269 were absolutely jubilant. The winds now were light, and the swells, while still 4 to 6 feet, were hardly felt on the barge. Small groups of men gathered around the bulletin board outside the radio room to read the weather updates posted every four hours. As they confirmed for themselves that Roxanne was just a storm and was still heading away from them, they laughed to each other. They had dodged another bullet. The 269 and her escorts had outlasted two hurricanes in three weeks and now the season was almost over. Seldom were there any hurricanes in the Gulf after October, and with any luck—and weren't they *due* for some luck?—they wouldn't have to face another hurricane for maybe another eight months. Only a few superstitious pessimists with worried expressions had the audacity to mention that on Friday the thirteenth one should not trust to luck.

For many of the men, that day was also one of relaxation. Even the deck crew, while cleaning, scraping, and doing small repairs, could relax. The divers and their tenders checked and cleaned gear. The cooks prepared a good hot lunch. But really there was not much for most of the men to do before they returned to the work site. While they had been under tow they had maintained a position roughly 15 miles east of the main oil field over the preceding two and a half days. In fact from 1800 on the tenth to midnight on the twelfth, throughout the hurricane, their position had changed less than 10 miles and nearly all of that was north to south and back to north. The tugs had kept the 269 away from the oil platforms to the west and well away from coastal areas to the south and east.

Lunch was hearty. The men had their choice of broiled dorado or enchiladas. The main dishes were accompanied by a selection of broiled potatoes, tortilla fixings, cooked vegetables, refried beans, and, as always, mounds of fresh fruit. In deference to certain American palates the cooks went easy on the chilies and spices. Besides the dinner items there were scrambled eggs and sausage, fried potatoes, and an array of breads and cereals. Half the men were coming off the staggered night shift, which might run from 2230 to 1030, or from 0000 to 1200, depending on the job. The reason for staggering the twelve-hour shifts was to ensure that the 269 would never be untended and that at no time would work cease. With the exception of a few specialized positions like radio operator, which utilized only one man per shift, the 269 carried a large enough crew to make sure that people were always on the job. At the evening meal, for instance, only half the night shift ate at any one time. The rest remained at their posts.

For each meal there was a choice of hot entrees, which varied by day of the week. Tuesdays there would be spaghetti, Wednesdays *arroz con pollo*, and on Sundays a favorite: steak and chicken barbecued on deck. Besides the evening entrees, which were offered twice a day, breakfast was served at both main meals.

After eating, some men worked out in the exercise room; others walked the deck for exercise or went into the TV room and watched old movies, of which there was a fairly large selection. In the back of the mess hall poker games had started. Generally poker marathons could only take place in bad weather, when regular operations had shut down. Normally, with all those except divers working a twelve-hour shift, no one had the time or energy for anything more than just a few poker hands. Today was different. After their scrape with Hurricane Roxanne they were ready for some relaxation. Lee Lloyd was at one table with Rountree, two other divers, and two tenders. Richard Lobb eventually joined the game. This was the big-stakes table where you could lose two or three hundred dollars in four or five hours—too rich for most of the Mexican crew. At another table a low-stakes game was in progress with both Mexican and American players. Mexican crew members had games going at three other tables.

Few of the thirty-one Americans onboard the 269 spoke much Spanish, and only a small number of the Mexican crew, except for a few of the foremen, spoke more than a necessary minimum of English. For this reason alone there might have been little camaraderie between the two groups. But the two social groups had very different cultures and financial means. For the most part they did not understand one another or even attempt to bridge the gap. The exceptions were in the diving contingent, where the Mexican-American and Mexican dive personnel did hang around with their English-speaking counter-parts, and in a few other isolated cases where some-one spoke the other's language.

There was also separation by bunk rooms. All the rooms, except for a couple of private or semi-private quarters for the superintendent and captain, housed four, six, or eight men and were usually shared by men with the same work. The deckhands would be together, the divers, the cooks, and so on. There was no favoritism. Mexican and American personnel had exactly the same facilities and received exactly the same privileges. The major difference was in their pay. The divers' handlers made a minimum of $40,000 or $50,000 a year and the divers twice that much. The Mexican deckhands made the equivalent of $3,500 a year. Specialized Mexican employees might make double the pay of deckhands. Mexican foremen could make the equivalent of $10,000 or $12,000 a year. Of course there was envy over the income disparity. Nevertheless, most of the Mexican crew were delighted to have a full-time job with, for them, excellent living conditions. Many in their entire lives had never eaten so well, or lived in air-conditioned comfort, or had hot and cold running water. The work on the 269 was not difficult and they received their pay on time, so all in all they considered themselves fortunate.

While there might not have been a great deal of international camaraderie on the 269, there was little fighting. The prohibition of liquor and drugs seemed to maintain peace. That is not to say that booze and drugs weren't present, but their use was mostly furtive. According to crew members, a few pot smokers puffed away when and where they could. Some

Americans and a few Mexicans smuggled whiskey or tequila onboard, snuck in with supplies or brought by men coming back from leave. Still, even if a full-fledged alcoholic could pass muster while under the influence, he would have a hard time maintaining a steady supply at sea. Also, there was seldom any privacy and there were few secure places to hide anything of size. Anyone caught overindulging, whether Latino or Yankee, was given a one-way ticket home.

There was no question that if alcohol were accepted, bored men, after months at sea, would use it indiscriminately. Discipline and morale would plummet and with their disappearance would go the safety of the men on the 269, already working in one of the world's most dangerous occupational environments. The divers, particularly, owed their lives to those who tended them, and there was no room for screw-ups by those who monitored their complex life-support systems or who guided the movements of the diving bell and the giant cranes that moved massive sections of pipe and pieces of equipment adjacent to the helpless men on the bottom.

Marco Polo Ramirez Leon was one of those responsible for the divers' safety. Even though he was a diver himself, he was working mostly as a dive tender. His duties included maintaining the diving bell, checking all its systems, and making sure that everything on it worked. He also helped with the saturation chamber and other work while waiting for a chance to dive. He thought he was fully capable of doing any work the American divers were doing if he could get the chance. But the Americans had all the experience, so they were the ones chosen for nearly all the work. Marco Polo, named by a father enchanted with the ancient explorer, was small, with fine features and a clipped mustache. He had received a good education, including two years at the community college in Ciudad del Carmen, and spoke fluent English. Now, with nothing to do, he joined the observers gathered around tables of men playing dominoes, Uno, and other card games.

Another of those looking on was Raul Salabania Acosta, a valve technician whose primary function was to check and maintain the production valves on the lines carrying oil and gas from the drilling platforms to shore. He had been working on the 269 for more than ten years. Most days he and a few other technicians would be ferried by crew boat or supply boat to one of the nearby oil rigs that were connected to the pipeline on which the 269 was working. Water would be pumped through the line and its pressure would be measured on the rig and on the barge. Any loss of pressure indicated a leak that had to be repaired before the line could be put in service. All the valves and gauges also had to be tested. When Raul was not working on the lines, he did odd jobs on the barge, working as a roustabout, assisting in the galley, or even occasionally filling in as a welder.

Raul and his wife, Bruna, had been married for twenty years. They lived in a small house in Carmen, where they raised their family. Every time Raul was due to go back to sea, Bruna would become very nervous, sure that this time something bad would happen to him. While he was working offshore she would go daily to the cathedral to pray for his safety. Raul had never even considered that he might not be safe— until now. In the last few days he had begun to wear his life jacket everywhere, even to bed. As he made his way from the tables filled with men playing cards to the TV room, where others were flaked out watching an old western, he realized that he was not the only one who was worried. Some others also were wearing their life jackets, just in case. Although Roxanne had passed by, many men believed the 269 was no longer a safe vessel to be on.

According to Raul and others, the 269 had a history of leaks and assorted problems. During a northerly in 1989 while the 269 was under tow, she was hit by 30-foot seas that swept over her weather deck, carrying away one of the ventilators that aired the accommodation deck below. Massive amounts of seawater poured down the ventilator shaft as well as through a leaky stairwell door and through a leak at the base of the big crane. Seawater flooded the accommodation deck. Richard Lobb ordered the crew to use mattresses and foam pads to try to stem the leaks. They were only partially successful, but in any case the barge's pumps were able to keep her afloat until she was towed into Carmen for emergency repairs.

The previous winter the 269 had been hauled out in Veracruz to repair damage and leaking at the point where the stinger is attached to the transom, but nothing had been done to address another major problem. According to anchor operator Kevin Dumont, enough rust had formed in the bilges over the twenty-eight-year life span of the 269 that her bilge pumps frequently clogged and had to be taken apart and cleaned. Other crew members said that some pumps were too small and some discharge lines were undersized—only 2 ½ inches in diameter, hardly larger than what would be used on a yacht. In the case of anything more serious than the routine leakage that occurs in nearly all old vessels, the bilge pumps might not be capable of ejecting a large enough flow of water. Indeed, during Hurricane Opal new leaks had opened up in the bilge tanks. During the days immediately preceding Roxanne a leak had developed on the main deck above the radio room, and the emergency anchor hanging from a fair-lead on the bow had swung hard enough to puncture a hole in the exterior plating above the waterline, thereby allowing water to enter whenever the barge hit a wave or fell into a trough. Kevin Dumont later said that the 269's bilge pumps had to operate nearly continuously just to keep up with these leaks, and except for frequent downtime spent cleaning rust out of the pump filters, they were operating almost around the clock—just to keep water levels down from the already discovered leaks.

The crew says there were other problems, too. According to Chuck Rountree, many bulkheads and through-hull fittings had lost their watertight integrity. Other crew members said that seals around some watertight doors used to close off flooded compartments had disintegrated, rust had corroded entirely through areas on some interior doors and bulkheads, and holes cut through some bulkheads to run conduit had never been sealed. If these charges are true, it would have been very difficult to maintain watertight integrity within compartments when major flooding occurred.

If, in fact, all of these problems did exist, it's doubtful that the old 269 could have passed U.S. Coast Guard inspections, something she would periodically be required to do if she were based and working in U.S. territorial waters. There is no evidence that she ever underwent a government inspection in Mexico. According to C.C.C.'s parent company, C.F.C., the American Bureau of Shipping did certify that the 269 was seaworthy in 1995, awarding the vessel its highest rating.

None of these issues were on the minds of most of the 269's crew that Friday, October 13, 1995. They relaxed and enjoyed themselves, quite happy to be receiving paychecks while having good meals, watching TV, or playing cards. Roxanne was beginning to seem like a distant memory, just one more storm that they had survived and that had been relegated to dusty archives and official records.

Saturday dawned cloudy and with a slight increase in wind and swell from the previous day. Wind and seas increased through the morning, and the noon Wilkens report and the National Weather Service Advisory provided an explanation: Mid- and upper-level winds from the northwest were pushing a cold front down along the Texas coast, and this, in turn, was blocking Roxanne's path to the north. Tropical cyclonic storms feed on warm, moisture-laden air, so when Roxanne's supply of warm air vanished in the northerly direction she had been traveling, she stalled. Although she was still fed by warm, moist air, all of it was now coming from the south—and she was getting plenty of it, enough to turn her back into a hurricane. By noon her wind speed had reached 75 miles per hour. The log of the *Captain John* shows that at 1300, weather conditions had worsened. At their position, winds were 45 to 50 miles an hour and seas were from 10 to 12 feet. Roxanne was returning to life.

Saturday morning ushered in a more immediate problem, however. Shortly after sunrise someone discovered that the hydraulic room was flooded. Forward of the generator room, amidships on the machinery deck, this 40-foot-wide by 80-foot-long space housed not only many of the 269's huge pumps, but controls for all the hydraulic pumps scattered over the entire vessel. Why *this* space should be flooding, no one knew, and no one could figure out how to stop the water now rising at an alarming rate.

Immediately the order was given to assemble all the men on deck in their life jackets. Nervous and sleepy, the day watch stumbled out on deck cursing and complaining. Meanwhile the captain, repairmen, technicians, and engineers hurried to the hydraulic room. Already the water had nearly reached the bottom of the watertight doors. Quickly a decision needed to be made whether to seal the room or to allow flooding of the entire machinery deck. Once the watertight doors were sealed they could be reopened to allow men working in the space to leave, but if the water kept rising in the hydraulic room, the water pressure would prevent the doors from being shut again. That could lead to the flooding of the entire vessel. On the other hand, evacuating all personnel and sealing the space not only would eliminate the possibility of finding and repairing the cause of the leak, but would necessitate towing the 269 to a drydock in Veracruz or Tuxpan. That was unacceptable except as a last resort.

Men worked feverishly in the few minutes they had before a decision had to be made to seal the space. Every pump that could be brought to bear was set to pump water out of the room and still the level did not appreciably go down. Finally someone discovered that one of the large pump's controls had been reset incorrectly sometime during the night, and instead of pumping water out of the hydraulic room, it was pumping water *into* it.

By midmorning the emergency was over and everyone was told to stand down. The deck was strewn with hoses that had carried water overboard. Since no announcement was made about what had happened, many men thought there had been a fire. Others said there was a hole in the 269's bottom. The men dispersed, but if some of the crew had been edgy before, they were more nervous now. More and more of the men realized things were taking place onboard that were being kept secret from them. When the crew of a ship, totally dependent as they are for their survival on the integrity of their vessel, feel that they are being kept in the dark about major problems affecting their ship, they become uneasy and resentful, as these men were Saturday morning. Grumbling could be heard that disaster was going to befall them. Not all of the men onboard were concerned. Some still had confidence that everything would be all right.

While many of the fearful groused among themselves, almost no one had the courage to gripe to the captain, much less to Superintendent Lobb. Only one man complained, vociferously and from the beginning, to the foremen, to the captain, to the superintendent, and to anyone and everyone who crossed his path. Kevin Dumont, the thirty-three-year-old Cajun anchor operator, had been working on offshore barges all his adult life. As a youngster he had grown up learning about the vessels and the work as his family traveled around the Gulf of Mexico and to the Middle East to be near his father, a barge superintendent for McDermott. For the last year Kevin had been dividing his time among the 269 and two other barges, all working in the same oil patch. He was well aware of the deficiencies of the old barge and was fearful that it might not withstand another hurricane.

When Kevin had gotten out of bed that Tuesday evening, during the first day of the storm, he was getting ready to begin his night shift when he discovered that the 269 was not being taken to a safe port but simply being held against the seas by her two tugs— that the orders had been given to weather Roxanne at sea. Kevin was anguished. The next night, when the divers finally emerged from their sealed saturation chamber after the end of their emergency decompression, one of the first people they saw, other than the doctor and their dive tenders and supervisors, was Kevin. Lee Lloyd and Kevin were neighbors back in Louisiana. Lee asked him, "Kevin, what the hell is goin' on?"

"These motherfuckers are killing us. This son of a bitch is going down! Richard Lobb is putting us out of business."

During the next few days Kevin repeatedly questioned the two barge foremen, Carlos Mendez and Jim Vines. "Why the hell are we staying out in the field while two other barges are going into the bay?"

Their standard replies drove him wild. "Well, you know, Kevin, we have to follow orders."

Joey Halliday, one of the anchor foremen, told Kevin that Joe Perot had radioed Richard Lobb, "Tell

Mother" [Doug Hebert, the super of the *Sara Maria*, was nicknamed "Mother" because, in the eyes of some, he acted like a mother hen], "if that pussy doesn't want to ride out the storm to bring the frickin *Sara Maria* in with the *Mega Dos*." That is just what Mother did—with thick skin and due caution, saving the lives of the men on his vessel.

Kevin confronted Richard Lobb directly, asking him why they didn't take shelter in the bay with the other barges. According to Kevin, Richard answered, "This old barge rode the North Sea like you wouldn't believe. This hurricane is going to turn north. It won't affect us. Don't worry, I have everything under control. Just don't worry!"

The flat-bottomed barges did seem to ride well in the long swells of North Sea storms and also in some northerlies in the Gulf of Mexico. They did not ride well, however, in hurricane seas producing steep waves of short interval, such as had developed during Opal and are typical in shallow waters in heavy weather.

Kevin read the weather reports and he was not convinced that Roxanne would continue heading north, as the initial reports predicted. "There was a high-pressure area over the Rockies, and hurricanes are unpredictable. I had a gut feeling that it might turn around." Though Kevin was the most vociferous in his objection to riding out the hurricane at sea, his fear of the results of this course of action was shared by many. Increasing numbers of crew members chose to sleep curled up in niches in supply rooms or other enclosed spaces on deck for fear of being trapped in their bunks should the 269 suddenly sink in the night.

Saturday afternoon before dinner and during a lull in their marathon poker game, Lee Lloyd made his way toward the radio room. The mess hall, where they had been playing, was aft in the 269. It was flanked by two hallways running fore and aft, and directly astern of it, butted up against the transom, was the galley. Two other large spaces shared the stern of the ship. To the left of the galley was the laundry and to the right was the TV/recreation room. Lee turned right into a hallway running from left to right in front of the mess. On the other side of the hall were the captain's, the superintendent's, and the foremen's cabins. Then on each side of two long halls running toward the bow were all the cabins for the crew.

When Lee reached the long starboard-side hallway, running fore and aft, he turned left, heading forward. Halfway to the bow was the radio room, and outside it a group of men clustered reading the weather reports, one in Spanish and one in English, posted on opposite sides of the door into the radio shack. So many men were in front of him, some appearing agitated and many talking among themselves, that Lee had trouble getting close enough to read the noon English radio report. When he did read it, the signs were not good. The winds were continuing to build, and although Roxanne had not yet started her turn back to the south, that reversal was now predicted. Already the vessels were bucking 55- to 60-mile-an-hour winds and 12- to 14-foot seas and the report suggested that these conditions would get worse.

During the day and evening Saturday, certain men made frequent visits to the radio room. It had been posted off limits to the crew, so only a few authorized personnel heard the conversations that took place between the 269 and the head office in Carmen. A few facts pertaining to those discussions did leak out, however.

Joe Islas was Richard Lobb's trusted assistant. Joe was in charge of the 269's paperwork, making sure that all the necessary reports were sent and the vessel's log was maintained correctly. He also had other duties, such as assigning cabins and keeping track of the men aboard and where they slept. During the days preceding Sunday, October 15, Islas acted as Lobb's communications conduit. Much of his time was spent in the radio room forwarding Lobb's side of the conversation to the head office, then relaying their response to Lobb wherever he might be on the barge.

From Tuesday, October 10, straight through to Sunday, the fifteenth, there was constant communication between the 269 and the head office. And while it is certain that many topics were discussed in the radio communications, it is also certain that foremost among them was what to do with the 269, to tow her into a port—and if so, which one—or to keep her at sea.

The most important discussion that was witnessed Saturday evening took place not in the radio room, but in the tower. The tower was considered the 269's command post, and at about 2100 Saturday evening, Richard Lobb, Assistant Superintendent John Enriques, an engineer by the name of Ortiz, and Acting Captain Cantu were gathered there, together poring over a maritime chart of the area. The hurricane had reversed its course. At its present rate of speed it would be upon them again the following day. According to a crew member present in the tower, one man told the others, "If we go there [meaning Coatzacoalcos, not the closest port, but the safest port], we can make it." And another commented, "If we move we miss one day's pay." Someone else then said, "Orders from shore are that we must stay in the area, here. Mr. P [Perot] says that we should stay." The crewman said the men studying the chart seemed, for obvious reasons, afraid to stay at sea. But because the *head* office warned them against going into port, they were more reluctant to have the barge moved to a safe harbor. So the 269 would face Roxanne at sea again.

By midnight on Saturday, fed by the same tropical Gulf air and seas that had pulled her over the Yucatan in the first place, Roxanne was now on a track roughly parallel to and a hundred miles east of her northwesterly course up the Gulf two days earlier. This time she was headed southeast, directly toward the 269. And as she approached the shallower, warmer waters adjacent to the Yucatan Peninsula, her wind speeds began to climb.

Chapter Four

~≈~

DAWN THAT SUNDAY was ominous. Menacing black skies, even well after daylight, briefly exposed eerie reddish streaks near the eastern horizon. The bottoms of cumulonimbus were packed so tightly that they formed a dark layer from which came periods of heavy rain and a howling wind. The wind was tolerable; the seas were not. Mainly they were still coming from the northwest, but some appeared to be driven out of the southwest. The waves were abrupt, almost vertical, and even worse, they came so close together that the barge seemed to barely get down one crest into the trough before the next wave was crashing right on top of her. Spume blew continuously off wave tops, lashing the sea with giant white patches downwind from each crest.

The waves hitting the 269 had begun building momentum before Roxanne had again reached hurricane status and started heading south. Her winds, now gusting at between 80 and 90 mph, were themselves capable of producing waves whose height equaled half the wind speed, and with the unimpeded distance between her and the 269 the waves had a great fetch in which to develop. There was another significant factor affecting the waves that hit the barge and her attendant vessels. Roxanne's location Saturday was in an area with an average water depth of 2,000 fathoms, or 12,000 feet. To the south the sea bottom shoaled dramatically until at the 269's position it was less than 100 feet. As Roxanne's waves approached, the shallow water slowed them and they began to mass vertically. Their displaced energy changed their shape, making them higher and steeper. So the waves crashing against the 269 that Sunday were not only immense, some cresting at 40 feet, they were vertical walls of water. However, their height was not the worst part.

A vessel can easily ride over huge waves if they are gradually cresting and spaced far apart, as they often are in the open ocean. But when waves are steep and close together, a vessel, particularly a smaller one, is tossed over the crests so that her bow and then her stern come out of the water. She then plunges into the succeeding trough. The damage inflicted by this type of a sea is greatest when it hits the vessel from abeam, where the mass presents the most resistance to the wave. The "immovable object meets the irresistible force" works here—except that the "immovable" object may roll over.

Not only the type of waves hitting the 269 but their strength can hardly be imagined. A cubic yard of water weighs about 1,500 pounds. By the time Roxanne's waves reached the 269 they were moving at least at 30 miles an hour. A 100-foot-long segment of a 30-foot-high wave slamming into the barge would do so with a forward momentum generating more than 12 million pounds of force. And to the men on the 269, that was exactly what the waves felt like that were hitting them.

The 269 and her tugs had been pushed 4 miles southeast since midnight, and at 0600 they were 23 miles southeast of the Nohoch-A platform. Roxanne herself was no longer a distant stranger. Since midnight she had been heading steadily southeast at a beggar's pace, about 3 knots. Shortly after dawn she changed course slightly, to a heading of 180°. She was northeast of the 269 and less than 100 miles away, the worst place she could possibly be. A Northern Hemisphere hurricane, like Roxanne, usually produces weaker winds on its left-front side and stronger winds on its right-front side, exactly where the barge and her tugs were positioned. With Roxanne closing in on them from the north, oil rigs to the west, and destruction likely in the shallow waters to the south and east, they had no place to run. They were trapped. By Sunday morning it was evident to the men on the 269 and the two tugs that they were going to be in for it.

At 0845 the *Captain John*'s towline broke for the third time, and this was at the worst possible location, the snatch line. The 8-inch-thick nylon hawser had parted near the middle, and neither of the tugs nor the barge had any more spares. This meant they would have to run cable to cable using one of the 269's anchor wires and would no longer have the benefit of a shock-absorbing snatch line, acting like a rubber band, to buffer stresses on the tow cable. Riggers on the 269 began making an eye from the end of the port-bow anchor cable.

Men on the exposed afterdeck of the *Captain John* did likewise. The deckhands on the barge rigging the eye on their anchor line were in almost as much danger as the tug crew. Each time the 269's bow came down the crest of a wave, it would immediately slam into another wave, and the following crest would race over the foredeck in a wall of water. The dozen riggers working on the towline would leap behind any bit of shelter or try to hold onto something solid. Those who couldn't find shelter within the few seconds available or who couldn't maintain their hold on a rail or stanchion were knocked off their feet and swept down the deck. Sometimes they smashed against an anchor windlass, a chock, or another piece of deck gear. Other men were carried in a flood of water to a railing, which they frantically grabbed to keep from being washed overboard. In spite of near catastrophes and without suffering more than broken fingers, bruises, and banged heads, they were finally able to rig an eye in the anchor cable.

A heaving line that fit into a canister on a mooring-line gun was attached to a brass rod that loaded into the gun's muzzle. The gun, called a 45-70 after the caliber of its blank cartridge, carries a serious charge. With a mighty kick it can send a line spiraling more than 200 feet. But it was next to useless in the face of hurricane-force winds. Time after time, with an exploding bark, a line shot into the wind but was immediately blown back to one side or the other of the barge. Again and again, Robert Trosclair had to ram the throttles forward to keep the *Captain John*'s stern from going under the crashing bow of the *269*. A few times the rod and attached heaving line did snake over the tug's stern, only to be washed overboard before one of the crew could pounce on it.

Waves now were so high that as the 269 sank into a trough they would sizzle past the men on the heliodeck 40 feet above the waterline. Each time the heaving line went out from the bow of the barge and fell into the sea, and Trosclair would again back his tug just ahead of the menacing bow, which with one blow could sink his vessel, just push her right under. In seconds the sea would pour in and she and her crew would likely be trapped under the 269's hull. The scenario of a tug run over and trapped under her tow is one with which all experienced towboat crews are familiar, and the men on the *Captain John* realized only too well that they were just one miscalculation away from its happening to them.

To compound their problems, Trosclair was having trouble keeping the *Captain John*'s bow into the wind. As he backed down on the 269, the wind and seas would push his bow to one side or the other, and the tug would start to go broadside to the barge astern of them. Only rapid corrections of heavy throttle and hard rudders saved them. Then, once more, Trosclair would begin backing down toward the behemoth in his wake.

The men on both tug and barge persevered in trying to reconnect the towline. They knew that in the prevailing wind and seas the *North Carolina* could not keep the 269 in position by herself, nor was her single towline likely to hold for long. Many crew members on all three vessels were surprised that with the stresses it was undergoing it had not parted already. By noon the tug's crew had finally managed to secure the new tow cable, and the *Captain John* was back on station. It had taken more than three hours to replace the line and to rejoin tug and barge in the face of a hurricane that was now nearly on top of them, only about 75 miles away. The wind was gusting to 80 miles an hour, and seas were rising like mountains above the top of the two tugs' pilothouses, sometimes breaking on the boats and sending waves of water surging down their decks. While the *269* and her tugs battled Roxanne, far to the north the U.S. Gulf Coast was enjoying a peaceful Sunday morning.

Just after the Civil War ended, Charles Morgan, a Gulf Coast steamship operator, bought the bankrupt New Orleans, Appaloosas and Great Western Railroad at a sheriff's auction. The Appaloosas had operated from Algiers—just across the Mississippi from New Orleans—to Brashear, Louisiana. The lower Mississippi at that time was undredged, permitting only small boats to reach New Orleans. Brashear, on the other hand, was a deepwater port on the Atchafalaya River 90 miles west of New Orleans and only 25 miles' sailing from the Gulf. Morgan resurrected the railroad, and Brashear became a main port for his fleet of cargo and passenger steamers sailing to the major Gulf ports, as well as to Cuba and even to New York. In 1876, to honor the man who put it on the map, the city renamed itself after him.

Morgan City lost its steamship prominence when the Mississippi was dredged and opened as far as New Orleans to oceangoing steamers in 1879. However, in the twentieth century it regained some of its importance as a fishing port, home to a large shrimp fleet. There was even a celebration called the Louisiana Shrimp Festival, which was ushered in each year by the blessing of the fleet. The festival then turned into a citywide party centered on a gala Cajun dance called a *fais-do-do*. This was Cajun dancing at its best. You could, in one evening, do the swamp pop, dance to old-fashioned waltzes and two-steps so sentimental that your heart would nearly break, and, if you had at least a drop of Cajun blood, work up a mighty great thirst hopping to a zydeco chanka-chank. A good *fais-do-do* was not to be missed.

In the 1950s gushers from offshore oil drilling in the Gulf of Mexico produced what was then America's newest black-gold rush, and Morgan City, one of the sheltered harbors closest to the Gulf where waterfront land, and in fact all land, was still cheap, hit the jackpot as a premier oil-supply port. The new industry became so important to the city that the shrimp festival was renamed the Louisiana Shrimp and Petroleum Festival, and everyone locally is quick to reassure the visitor that, indeed, there is no incongruity: oil drilling has hardly killed any shrimp or other marine critters at all. Many of the shrimp fishermen who also have family members working in the offshore oil industry keep their lips tightly sealed on the subject—even though they know better.

In 1956 Morgan City took off when J. Ray McDermott established a major construction yard there dedicated solely to building offshore oil-drilling platforms. Then other big companies came wading in. Tidewater Marine, one of the world's largest operators of towing and supply vessels for the offshore oil industry, chose Morgan City as its principal Gulf port and brought in more than 200 vessels. Two large commercial diving companies, Oceaneering International and Cal-Dive International, set up bases of operations, employing between them nearly 1,500 people. And for every large company that came to Morgan City, dozens of smaller ones sprang up too.

One of the smaller companies, North Bank Towing, dates back to 1956, when Sam Smith, a local boy, started its predecessor, the F&S Boat Company, with his one and only tug, the *Saratoga*. North Bank grew along with the industry it supplied. In 1995 it had 19 vessels, nearly all tugs and oil-supply boats, though it did own one geophysical research ship, and it still operated from Morgan City.

On the morning of October 15 the *Miss Robin*, one of North Bank's tugs, was quietly moored at a fuel dock on Bayou Boeuf, a branch of the Atchafalaya River, just south of Morgan City. As always, single-sideband chatter blared out on 8 megahertz, the frequency most used for calls to and from North Bank vessels. Shortly after 1200 a call came in for the *Miss Robin* from the *Captain John*. It happened that Robert Trosclair Jr., the son of the *Captain John*'s master, was aboard and received it. The senior Robert asked his son to call Chuck Denning, North Bank's manager, at home and ask him to immediately go down to the company office so that Robert could talk to him over single-sideband. It was urgent. Robert Jr. called Chuck at home and passed on the message.

Chuck Denning is a stocky, good-natured forty-seven-year-old Louisianian who has tugboats in his blood. He has worked on and around them most of his adult life and has owned and managed them since 1978. Now that Sam Smith is pretty much retired, Chuck runs the show. After he received Robert Jr.'s call he raced down to the company's modest office, a remodeled bungalow sitting on the west bank of the

Atchafalaya in the Morgan City suburb of Berwick.

Denning had already been to the office. That Sunday at 0700 he had checked in by radio with all his tugs that were working or were at sea. When he had spoken with Robert Sr. on the *Captain John* at about 0730, Robert told him they were going through heavy seas associated with the return of the hurricane but that everything seemed under control. Chuck then went home to enjoy his Sunday morning breakfast. Now, obviously, the situation had changed.

When he got back to the office, Chuck immediately went to the single-sideband transmitter in the radio room. "KZJ930 Morgan City base to Whiskey-Charlie-Yankee 5568. *Captain John, Captain John.* Come on in, *Captain John.*"

A long pause, then "This is Whiskey-Charlie-Yankee 5568, *Captain John*, back to KZJ930."

"Robert, *Miss Robin* called me, and they say you have a problem." And Robert began telling his boss what was confronting the *Captain John*, the *North Carolina*, and especially the 269. The towline had broken again. The crew was repairing it and they hoped to be back on station soon, but even with both vessels towing, they were not able to maintain their position. They were losing ground steadily, being pushed to the southeast at better than 3 knots. And, to make matters worse, according to word they had received from the barge, the 269 had developed some serious leaks.

The leaks that had started weeks before, during Hurricane Opal, were centered in the starboard compressor room directly forward of the transom on the stern of the 269. While previously the pumps had been equal to the task of keeping up with the water coming in, by Sunday morning they no longer were. By 1000, leaking had increased and water was coming into two adjacent compartments. By 1100, even with watertight doors closed, water had spread to five compartments on the stern. Then it began seeping up through the floor of the recreation room on the deck above the original leaks. Each time the 269 rode up a wave, her stern was buried in the preceding trough and seawater would slam against the vulnerable transom, perhaps enlarging the cracks that had already formed. The leakage flow seemed to increase by the hour.

All but the latest sleepers had already had their breakfasts when at about 1000 the call went out all over the 269 in both Spanish and English for all personnel to immediately assemble, wearing their life jackets, at their respective life-raft stations. Men dropped whatever they were doing and rushed to their quarters for their life jackets, then scrambled topside. Mexicans and Americans debated among themselves as they congregated at their life stations about the reason for this latest turnout. Rumors of leaks all over the vessel had spread among them. Some men looked down at the sea, trying to gauge whether the 269 was sinking, but most kept away from the rails and the possibility of being swept overboard.

Lee Lloyd had already eaten but was still in the mess hall enjoying a last cup of coffee when the order went out. Immediately he went to his room and put on his wetsuit top and a dive shirt. He grabbed his wallet with his previous two days' poker winnings, which amounted to nearly $800, stuffed it, his wristwatch, and a dive knife into a waterproof bag, and headed up the ladder to the main deck. As he went up, whom should he see but Kevin Dumont rushing the other way carrying a tool kit, obviously going to some problem area. Kevin was a master mechanic who could fix nearly anything and had been called down to help. Because of his job he would know what was going on. "Dumont," Lee queried, "how does it look?"

Kevin paused half a second in his rush to get below. "It don't look good, bro," he rasped.

"Whatchu mean?" Lee rasped back.

"It don't look good!" was the only reply he heard over Kevin's shoulder as he disappeared below.

Shane Richins, another diver, was one of the late sleepers. He remembered a dive tender coming into the room he shared with three other dive personnel and waking them up, yelling, "Hey, you guys need to get your life jackets and come up on deck. They want everybody on deck." Shane jumped into his clothes, grabbed his life jacket, and, still mostly asleep, ran up on deck with the others. Not thinking that the barge would sink, he didn't bother taking his wallet, watch, and other valuables—a lapse he later regretted. He reached the deck to see 200 guys milling around, wondering in both Spanish and English what the hell was happening. The wind was blowing the waves so hard that the spray off the wave crests hit him like pellets blasted out of a shotgun.

Most of the dive crew congregated on the helicopter deck just forward of the big gantry crane near the stern. From their vantage point 40 feet above the water they had a good view of nearly everything taking place. The 269 was being held bow to the seas by the *North Carolina*, but even under tow the two vessels were being driven backward.

Towing the 269 in a hurricane was like trying to tow Grand Coulee Dam. With her massive crane, helicopter deck, and high sides, the barge acted like a big steel sail. Each time the *Captain John* backed down in front of the barge in an attempt to reconnect the towline, the men on the deck of the 269 expected a collision that would finish the tug, and maybe them too, because the impact would certainly be enough to break their remaining towline to the *Carolina*. With nothing to hold the barge's bow into the seas, the 269 would go broadside. And if that happened, she would certainly roll over.

Meanwhile, below deck the 269's engineering crew had every available pump operating. The water level in the bilges was alarmingly high, and water was rising in all the machinery spaces aft. Efforts had failed to eliminate any of the leaks, and new ones seemed to have started at the base of the big crane. The crane's mass and weight above deck, heaving with the vessel to which it was attached, created substantial stresses on the structural members supporting it below deck level. A steel beam pushed just millimeters out of place could pull deck plates with it that might allow seawater to enter. Then, traveling between decks and moving with each pitch of the barge through cracks in ceilings and interior bulkheads, small- to medium-sized leaks could collectively allow vast quantities of water to penetrate what were supposed to be watertight spaces.

In an old vessel like the 269, which in her nearly twenty-eight-year history had taken numerous beatings at sea and had undergone many repairs, leaks could form at any stress points, and water could then be carried through the vessel via the numerous conduits containing all the barge's wiring. These conduits are always plugged with stuffing during a ship's construction for the express purpose of preventing water that might have entered a vessel at any point from being carried through the entire ship. Unfortunately, because the stuffing impedes rewiring, it is usually torn out by electricians doing repairs or electrical upgrading and is seldom replaced. There is no certainty that this was the case on the 269, although it is common practice. In any case, holes had been cut through bulkheads for wiring or other purposes and had never been closed, according to Chuck Rountree. What with the possibility of leaking conduits, and with the poorly sealed watertight doors and leaking bulkheads, seawater was being carried throughout the vessel. Another means by which leaks can spread is the heating/air-conditioning system, but since the 269 had few air-conditioned spaces on its machinery deck, this had not been an immediate concern. However, now that water levels were reaching the living quarters on the deck above, it was a recipe for catastrophe.

In the supply room Gustavo's shift had started at midnight and was due to end at noon, when El Padre would take over. Saturday night had begun slowly.

With the barge under tow, few calls were made for equipment. Gustavo had his assistants check the lashings on all the larger equipment and made sure the screen doors on the enclosures for small items were also secured. Sunday morning, however, was a different story. Men began rushing in for hoses and pump connections. As soon as they received what they came for, they went tearing back out, calling to Gustavo that it was an emergency and they didn't have time to fill out paperwork. If he didn't like it, he could talk to Señor Lobb.

What was happening was all too clear to Gustavo and to everyone else on the barge, so it was no surprise when everyone was told to put their life jackets on and assemble on deck. Before Gustavo and his men could shut down and leave the storeroom, one of the barge foremen came in and ordered all of them to put out as many buckets and water containers as they could find. There was a considerable number, and as soon as they were stacked at the supply room entrance, a group of men came down and carried off as many as they could handle. When all the available buckets were put out, Gustavo and his assistants were ordered to follow the others aft.

The pumps could no longer keep up with the water flowing into spaces near the stern on the machinery deck. Perhaps a bucket brigade would make enough difference to keep them afloat. Over a hundred men had been ordered to form two lines extending from the stern on the machinery deck going up the stairwell leading to the galley. The lines of men ended at the drain in the washing area. Furiously men passed two-thirds-full buckets up one line and empties back down the other. The water from the buckets, once emptied in the drain, was pumped over the side. The grand plan came to nothing. The bucket brigade didn't seem to make any difference at all. The water level kept rising. After an hour and a half, the men were told to stop and to go topside.

In the recreation room welders were trying to seal the hatch in the deck through which water was gushing from the filled compressor room below it. Evidently the water pressure in that space, sealed with watertight doors, was so great that it was forcing open cracks and seams in bulkheads and the ceiling. Even using an arc welder, the welders failed to seal the hatch. Superintendent Lobb then ordered mattresses and foam pads to be laid over the hatch cover in a desperate attempt to staunch the flow of water into the rec room. The watertight doors that were leaking could still slow the flooding's advance on the machinery deck, but the living-quarters deck contained few watertight doors. Also, even if there had been watertight doors in every space, the heating/air-conditioning ducts would allow water to be carried to every compartment on the entire deck. More and more mattresses were stacked on the floor of the rec room and still the water gushed in. This proved to be another failure, and now there seemed to be few, if any, options remaining.

By early afternoon another leak had developed on the starboard side, forward, perhaps in a ballast tank beneath the machinery deck. Water began flowing into the desalination room above it, and the 269 began listing further to starboard as water collected on that side.

As the morning had progressed, some of the men had stayed at their life-raft stations. Others had tried to find some shelter from the furious wind, which not only tore at them but blew spray and rain in blinding, stinging sheets, horizontally and continuously. The men began to suffer teeth-chattering cold, and in the tropics they were not prepared for it. The Mexican crew, many of whom wore only skimpy shirts and jeans, suffered the most. Most of the divers and some of the dive-support crew had put on wetsuit tops before coming on deck and so were relatively well protected. Even they, however, looked for sanctuaries more sheltered than the exposed heliodeck. Some of the dive crew retreated to a semiprotected walkway next to the superstructure of the big crane and below the heliodeck. From their new vantage point they had a good view of the end of the pipe alley where it dropped diagonally into the sea at the 269's stern. From the end of the alley the finished pipeline was lowered to the seabed on a long steel tail, called a stinger, which hinged on the transom and had been removed and lashed to the deck prior to Roxanne's first arrival. Hour after hour the men watched the sea level creep up the diagonal pipe alley, mute testimony to the fact that their vessel was sinking.

The men, even those on deck, began to hear strange noises. Ray Pepperday, a muscular twenty-five-year-old saturation technician, kept all the specialized dive gear working. He remembered standing with the other dive staff, listening. "I started hearing a lot of noises internally, you know, structural creaking and then popping and stuff. The five years I had worked on that barge I had never heard anything like that. Being relatively new compared to some of the other guys like Mr. Cobb, he's been in it for years, I'd more or less talk to him. 'Well, what do you think the odds are of this thing sinking?' On my part there was a lot of disbelief. I just didn't think that, with the time I'd spent on these vessels, in my mind, it just wasn't gonna sink."

Neither Lenn Cobb nor any of the other experienced men who had worked for decades on the barges, and who had seen them survive terrible storms time after time, thought at first that the 269 was going to sink. But as the day wore on they began to change their minds.

Most of the Mexican crewmen were huddled near their life-raft stations. Some were praying. Others were simply sitting with hollow, vacant stares, almost in shock. For the most part the Mexicans were not seafarers, but welders and general laborers from the Yucatan interior who were as unfamiliar with the sea and ships as they might have been with outer space if they had been shot into it. In most cases they had stood in employment lines week after week in hopes of finding a steady job with regular pay—any job. Many had little experience with hurricanes at sea, and most of them now thought they were going to die.

Ray Pepperday, Marco Polo, and some of the other dive crew spent part of Sunday running around giving the Mexicans a crash course on how to wear their life jackets. Some had tied the jackets around their necks, and if they had snagged the jacket on something, they would have hanged themselves. Lionel, a good-natured young Mexican dive tender, had decided to accompany the divers, many of whom he was friendly with. Lee Lloyd saw him sitting in a corner shivering. Lionel gave Lee a scared smile as he walked by. Lee stopped and peeled off the long-sleeved heavy dive shirt he was wearing over his wet-suit top, then gave it to Lionel, who put it on with a happy nod of gratitude. As the day progressed, members of the dive crew would walk around the base of the big crane on the walkway that encircled it, pointing out to each other changing conditions on the ocean or on the barge itself. Tim Noble and some of the divers moved inside the dive shack at the base of the crane, where they sat out of the weather, talking and smoking and analyzing their situation.

Lee Lloyd was more cautious. He didn't join the divers inside the dive shack. "I would not go in there or go below deck" (during the day some of the crew ran below to the galley and grabbed handfuls of cookies or whatever was there, since no food had been handed out since breakfast). "I thought that son of a bitch [the 269] might roll over and I was not going to be trapped inside. So I stayed outside. My whole focus at that time, and for the whole ten hours that day, was putting myself in the best position that I could to give me the best chance to survive. The whole day I thought that barge was going to roll over, and I thought, well, if it rolls this way, then I'll go that way—or if this [piece of equipment] breaks loose, then I'm going to do that."

Some others tried to weigh their options and to

position themselves as best they could to survive a sinking, but most just waited for orders.

The inner harbor at Ciudad del Carmen is protected with a high rock breakwater. That Sunday morning the *Ducker Tide* was safely tied to the dock in her berth there. The crew had just finished making breakfast, delighted not to be at sea in conditions with which they were all too familiar. The *Ducker* is a 190-foot combination supply/anchor/towboat almost exactly like the *North Carolina*. It is owned by Tidewater Marine, the largest American provider of vessels to the offshore oil industry. The *Ducker's* captain, Harold Roche, had been operating towboats for over a quarter century and was considered one of the best in the business.

Harold himself took the call. It was from Pemex Offshore, the section of the giant Mexican national oil company that handled the operations of vessels working its marine oil fields. The dispatcher asked Harold if the *Ducker* could take diesel to two small self-propelled barges caught outside with not enough fuel to reach port. The captains of the two vessels were threatening to beach them in the face of the hurricane. Harold and a very unhappy crew stuffed down the last of their breakfasts, threw off the *Ducker's* lines, and headed into the storm.

Harold found the two barges and, in spite of large waves smashing his vessel, was able to refuel one barge, then the other, without incident. Satisfied that he and his men had done their good turn, they headed back to Carmen as fast as sea conditions would allow. They almost made it, too. They had just passed the sea buoy marking the beginning of the channel and were minutes from reaching the security of their berth when another call came in, again from Pemex Offshore. The 269 was in jeopardy. Could they go to her aid? There were no other boats that could help out.

Over VHF Harold called some of his fellow captains whose vessels were berthed in Carmen. Hell no, they were not taking their boats out. The hurricane was headed right for them. He was crazy if he went back out. Even the Mexican Navy wasn't moving. Harold thought of the hundreds of men onboard the barge and made his decision. He swung the *Ducker* around and headed back out to sea. His crew despaired, but they had faith in their captain and no alternative in any case.

When the *Captain John* finally reestablished its towline, Robert Trosclair was able to talk to Chuck Denning over single-sideband. Robert told his boss that with no more snatch lines to absorb the stresses on the tow and anchor cables connecting tug and barge, he doubted that their towline would last long. It lasted almost exactly one hour. When it parted again at 1300, the cable leading to the *Captain John* from the 269 broke where it went through the chock to the barge's port-bow winch drum. By this time massive waves swept by them, some 40 feet high. The wind shrieked and gusts were clocked at 90 miles an hour. Trosclair decided that under the existing conditions it was too dangerous to once again risk the lives of his men to try to reestablish the towline. He reported his decision to Richard Lobb on the barge and to Chuck Denning, now riveted to the single-sideband in North Bank Towing's office in Morgan City. *Derrick Lay Barge 269* and the 245 men onboard her were hanging on to a last thread of control: the remaining towline to the *North Carolina*.

Chapter Five

❧

BY EARLY AFTERNOON the 269 had taken on so much water that she was sitting lower in the sea. This helped to dampen the rolling that had occurred earlier in the day, but she was now more vulnerable to breaking waves. Each time a wave hit, it was as though a giant's fist had slammed into her, crashing, exploding, and sending a shudder through the entire vessel. Some wave tops began sweeping across her deck and things began to break loose. Even before equipment had begun breaking free, the deck gang had been ordered to tie down all the gear. Extra lines were wrapped, chains were more securely fastened, and care was taken to see that everything topside was well secured.

The young deckhand Luis Domingo was working

with three others just forward of the big crane. Four of the eight sea buoys used to carry the tugs' pickup lines to the 269's anchors lay on the port side, two forward and two aft. Each of the 10-foot-long buoys was about 4 feet in diameter and weighed about 1,700 pounds. In normal weather their steel cradles prevented them from rolling around the deck. But not now. A welder bent over one of the buoys, laboriously welding a pipe bracket to hold it in place. However, at the rate he was welding, it would take him two days to do all eight, so the foreman had ordered the deck-hands to lash the others down.

Using 2-inch line, Luis Domingo and the rest of the deck gang worked feverishly to tie the buoys in their cradles. As waves broke against the 269 the men became soaked with spray. They had already been on deck since early morning with little or nothing to eat. Some men, fearful that the 269 would sink at any moment, had also spent the previous night on deck. They had preferred being cold topside, huddled under blankets in various niches, to being trapped below deck if the barge should go down during the night.

Luis Domingo had not thought of this possibility, so he had slept soundly in his bunk. But he was sure thinking of it now. As the day progressed, he became more and more fearful. He tried to get reassurance from the older men in the deck gang, but they just shook their heads. It was in God's hands. Just before noon, already shivering with cold, Luis Domingo raced down to his quarters and grabbed his old nylon windbreaker. He dashed into the galley and helped himself to a handful of cookies laid out for whoever wanted them. Then he scrambled back on deck, where he remained, wishing he'd gotten one of the shore jobs he'd applied for.

No matter how well the deckhands had secured things, it seemed like they might as well have saved the effort. The waves rolled across the deck with such force that as each hit, something else broke loose. The dozen deckhands were divided into three gangs. Chains and more rope were put out by the foreman, who ordered them again to try to secure everything that was slopping back and forth.

Luis Domingo did not know the guy he was working with. They had not said ten words to each other in the past. Now the two of them looked at each other in terror. They were being sent to their deaths. Already two of the sea buoys that they had just finished tying down had broken their lashing and were washing from side to side with each roll of the barge. They approached the buoys slowly, trying to gauge where they were likely to roll next. If they got too close and a big wave hit the barge, they would be squashed like beetles. A second glance at each other conveyed their simultaneous decision: To hell with the buoys. They turned their attention to some of the smaller gear that sloshed back and forth. Fortunately, before long, one of the buoys plunged over the side. Two others took its place, careening like crazy to port and then back to starboard. Four other deckhands tried to grab one and hold it while the other two men in their gang wrapped lines around it. All of them were whipped like rag dolls and pulled off their feet by the buoy as a big wave swept it along the deck. One of the men only narrowly escaped being crushed.

Then, two 4,000-pound rolls of fill-joint material, actually galvanized tin, broke loose and started smashing into everything around them. Each time they crashed into something, they would carry away whatever they hit. Four other deckhands carrying chains chased after the cylinders in a frightened dance of nervous approach and terrified retreat according to the movement of the rolls. They managed to chain one to a winch; the other slipped harmlessly over the side. Trying to capture huge pieces of rolling equipment had become impossible, and even the foreman realized it. He ordered the deck gangs to stop their work and leave the area before someone was killed. The men congregated forward, in the lee of the small crane. The foreman scrawled notices, "Danger—Do Not Enter," in Spanish on the backs of some small metal signs. Two men were given the signs and some rope and told to string them across the deck two-thirds of the way aft.

No sooner had the men left the area than a big wave tore two decompression chambers from their brackets. The chambers, basically just large hollow pipes, had been closed and pressurized in preparation for the bad weather to prevent seawater from seeping in. The pressurization had the unintended effect of making them buoyant. The ton-and-a-half steel chambers were tossed around like matchsticks, mingling with an alarming amount of other debris in a sloshing junk pile on deck.

The decompression chambers were by no means the most hazardous of the flotsam, however. Unbelievably, many oxygen bottles had been stored in wicker baskets. The baskets began to disintegrate when the dozen 200-pound oxygen bottles inside them were thrown from side to side. Soon, 4-foot-high oxygen bottles were also rolling around on deck. The empty bottles were no major threat, but the filled ones, under 3,000-pounds-per-square-inch pressure, were unguided missiles. A filled oxygen bottle, when its valve has been hit, has been known to blast right through the hull plating of a ship. In one shipyard accident a bottle went through the outer hull of a ship being worked on and exploded in the space between the two hull walls, killing two workers who happened to be laboring inside. Some of the loose bottles on the 269 rolled overboard harmlessly. Others whose valves smashed into something solid produced a deafening shriek and took off, screaming rockets that blasted into the air or ricocheted off the crane tub, a deck-house, or an anchor windlass before hurtling overboard without hitting anyone.

Some of the life rafts also deployed after their canisters were hit by waves. The 10-foot-diameter rafts would suddenly inflate and immediately be lifted into the sky, flying saucers, never to be seen again. All had tethers that were supposed to prevent deployed rafts from being lost, but the tethers were no match for the winds, which parted them in the blink of an eye.

With the deck becoming more and more dangerous and the wind continually blowing wave tops and spray, men huddled in or under whatever shelter they could find. Some of them, mostly dive personnel, had retreated to the second floor above the saturation chamber, which contained the room where all the diving-climate and gas controls were monitored. Sitting forward of the big crane and a story and a half above the main deck, with doors leading out in different directions, it seemed like a relatively safe place to hang out.

Ray Pepperday, who was with those in the sat building, occasionally stepped into the corridor next to the doorway leading to the stern to see what was going on. A Mexican rigger foreman stood by the door with a hand-held radio. He had been stationed there because it was the only safe vantage from which he could look down and see everything happening on the stern. Pepperday and the foreman would exchange a few words, but since neither could speak the other's language, they were limited in their communication. Together they would watch a big sea push the 269 over on her side, and as she listed, the foreman would talk into his walkie-talkie, reporting on conditions and damage. On one of his trips to the doorway, Ray stood looking over the foreman's shoulder as the 269 rolled over a wave and sank into the next trough. The barge seemed to groan, then listed heavily to starboard, the side the two men were on. Both men saw the next wave. Even a story and a half above deck, they watched it towering over them, and there was nothing between it and them but one open door. Pepperday turned and ran for his life down the corridor. It was 15 feet long and 8 feet wide near the doorway but narrowed to 3 feet just before it turned left leading to the sat control room. The last thing

Pepperday remembers before he was hit by the water was noticing that somehow the watertight door behind him had closed after the wave hit, sealing and pressurizing the space. The wave bowled him head over heels into the cramped space at the end of the corridor. Picking himself up in the pitch-black hallway, Pepperday heard the foreman behind him screaming.

Ray waded back to the door. Evidently the foreman had tried to close the door but hadn't managed to close it entirely before the wave hit or been able to retract his hand in time. His hand and most of his forearm were on the outside of the steel door, now completely closed. Ray remembers thinking, "'He's caught in there and he's comin' completely unglued.' I tried to kick the door open. I tried and tried and I couldn't do it. So I ran back through the corridor to where all the guys were. They had been hit pretty good and were still trying to pick themselves up. I shouted for help and headed back to the outside door where the foreman was still stuck. By this time he had gone into shock. He just stared a blank stare."

Ray and Shane Richins tried kicking the door in unison, but something had wedged it shut. Finally, kicking together, they got it to let go. As it went flying open they heard something big go wham, wham,

wham, bouncing down the steps leading to the next deck. A 5,000-pound portable hydraulic plant had been picked up from the lower deck by the wave and jammed against the door. Fortunately it was not sitting flat against the door or the two men would never have been able to dislodge it.

Amazingly, the foreman had not passed out. He had suffered a compound fracture, and where the skin had not been broken, it immediately started to fill with blood. "We were trying to get him out of there," Ray remembers, "and my Spanish is limited, so I didn't know how to ask him how badly he was hurt. I stuck my hand in his face and I wiggled my fingers, you know, 'Try it.' I'll be damned if this guy didn't look down at his hand and wiggle his fingers. Then we got him the hell out of there—walked him off down to the bow area out of harm's way." Ray figured that losing the use of his arm would cut down on the foreman's chances of coming through alive if they were told to abandon ship. He looked for the foreman later but saw no sign of him again that day, either dead or alive.

From the tower that Sunday, Kevin Dumont watched the whole drama unfolding below. He had spent Saturday night there, hardly able to sleep, so sure was he that the 269 was going to sink. As he said later, "I wasn't going to get trapped in that son of a bitch." With fear turning to anger and then sadness, Kevin witnessed his vessel slowly going down beneath him. Sometimes he was alone, sometimes with others. Another tower operator, Steve Howell, came in around noon. He sat down on an overturned five-gallon plastic bucket, shaking his head at the devastation. The slim forty-five-year-old anchor operator was from Mississippi, where he still lived with his wife and children. Following his father into the offshore construction business, Steve had been working on barges for more than twenty years. He had loved the work and the life on the water, but now he was as scared as everyone else.

Kevin was a devout Catholic. Steve was quickly becoming one. "Steve," Kevin said, "let's say a prayer." "I know one," Howell replied. They clasped hands and prayed together.

Kevin hadn't eaten since early morning, and it seemed unlikely that they would get food any time soon. So at about 1230 he took a chance and ran down to the galley. It was a madhouse. Men who had not eaten since breakfast were frantically grabbing any food they could find and stuffing it in their mouths before racing back on deck. Kevin slapped together some roast beef sandwiches to take up to the tower for himself and Steve and the other two anchor operators. Two foremen and Alvarez Cantu, the captain, visited the tower off and on, but they weren't there when Kevin returned. Rozy—Ronald Rozmarynoski, the sat technician—came in shortly afterward. He and Kevin were good friends, and they commiserated over what they viewed as the needless sinking of the 269.

As the 269 settled even deeper in the water, more of the crew congregated on the narrow walkway that ringed the tower, until by the middle of the afternoon fifty to seventy-five men were wrapped around it. Richard Lobb periodically came in to the tower too, since it gave the best vantage point short of climbing up the big crane. Kevin watched Lobb surveying the destruction taking place. "He saw the wave size. He saw what was going on. He saw everything he needed to see. His eyes were like he was going through hell." One of the foremen came into the tower and reported to Lobb, "Boss, the stern is not recovering."

Lobb nodded. Earlier in the day when a wave hit the stern, it would push that end of the 269 down but the vessel would bob back up as the wave passed. So much water now flooded the spaces aft that the stern was no longer coming back up.

Addressing the men in the tower, Lobb asked, "Where is the third boat? Has anybody seen the third boat? Have you made a visual with her?" No one had seen the *Ducker Tide*, which they could only hope was on her way to give them assistance.

At about 1400, to ease the strain on the last towline holding the 269 to the *North Carolina*, the order was given to drop the barge's two huge bow anchors. The port anchor cable had just been reaffixed to the anchor chain that earlier had broken away from the *Captain John*. When the bow anchors were let go, the port anchor went to the bottom. The starboard anchor did not. Evidently the anchor pendant, a cable attached to the anchor and used to haul it up to the tug as part of the anchor-raising process, fouled in the towing bridle.

In an instant, the 269's mass was no longer distributed directly behind the *North Carolina*; the bridle now carried the weight of the starboard bow anchor not in the center, but all on one side. Immediately, the towing cable, instead of going directly astern of the *North Carolina*, swung to her starboard quarter until it caught on the starboard towing bitts. The supply boat careened on her starboard beam-ends, and before anyone could do anything, she started to roll over.

A tug girded, or capsized, by her tow is one of the greatest hazards of towing. Most modern towing vessels have quick-release systems that allow their crew, with the push of a button or the throw of a lever, to release their tow cable. The *North Carolina* had such a system, but everything happened so quickly that no one could activate it.

Eulalio Zapata, the first mate, and two of the crew who happened to be on deck were thrown into the bulwarks, and nearly into the sea. They hadn't even time to brace themselves. One second the *North Carolina* was relatively stable and the next she was rolling over. The sea whipped over a third of the deck and water began pouring into the aft companionway leading to all the interior spaces.

Eulalio regained his feet and started trying to wade toward the towing drum and the cable-release lever, but he was too late. The *Carolina* was within one or two seconds of a total capsize, and neither Eulalio nor anyone else could stop her. Suddenly, with a crack, her tow cable parted and instantly she bobbed upright. Eulalio and the deckhands looked at each other in amazement. They had just escaped death.

As the 269's anchors hit bottom, cable was allowed to play out to provide as much scope as possible without allowing so much that the barge's lateral movement would twist one cable over the other. However, when the brakes were thrown on the anchor windlasses to slow, then stop, the play of cable, nothing happened. The barge was traveling backward so rapidly that the windlass brakes could not slow the rush of cable. Clouds of smoke poured out of the windlasses as the brake friction bands burst into flames. Finally all the cable played off the drums and splashed into the sea. The barge now was adrift and she, too, was seconds away from rolling over.

Forward ballast tanks had been filled earlier in an attempt to raise the 269's sinking stern and to stem the intrusion of seawater, but this made little difference in her trim. Besides the usual weight of her big crane, there was too much water already in her machinery deck. Also, waves had been surging over the stern incessantly, adding even more weight aft. She was so heavily weighted aft and so much of her stern was below water that the 269 acted like a big sea anchor.

As soon as the bow anchor cables were lost, the barge whipped around 180° until her stern was directly into the waves. That she simply did not go broadside to the seas and roll over was a miracle in itself and was attributable to the sea-anchor effect of the sunken stern. If, even for a minute, she had remained broadside to the enormous seas that were hitting her, she would have rolled over and sunk, just as her sister the *DB-29* had done years earlier off the South China coast.

As soon as her stern faced the seas, both stern

anchors were let go, but this action, too, accomplished nothing. As wind and waves pushed her toward the southeast, probably at better than 6 knots, the two cables snapped the moment their anchors caught on the bottom. The 269 was again completely adrift, and this time nothing could prevent her from sinking.

On deck Ray Pepperday was standing with Ricky Perez, a dive tender, when Danny Miller, the vessel's electrician, came up from below. Ricky told him, "You look like you've been through the ringer." Danny nodded. "It ain't gonna be long before we lose the generator room. We can't stop the water comin' in." With that Danny wiped the sweat off his forehead and went below again. Sure now that the 269 was going down, Ricky ran back to his room one last time and a few minutes later came back with a briefcase containing his valuables. Superintendent Lobb happened to see him and said, "Well, you can forget bringing that with ya." Undaunted, Ricky produced a Ziploc bag, put his money, watch, and passport in it, and taped it to his body with gaffer's tape.

Below deck some of the barge's crew still toiled to keep the pumps running, but to no avail. Water in the spaces adjacent to the transom had reached the ceiling, and water gushed through the hatch in the deck of the TV room directly above. Water then began spreading like an uncontrollable plague into the other living spaces. With no watertight doors on the quarters deck, the spread of the flooding now could not be stopped.

At 1615 the 269's radio operators sent what turned out to be the final distress message. It was transmitted to C.C.C. headquarters in Carmen and to Pemex Offshore. It informed the recipients that *Derrick Lay Barge 269* was in imminent danger of sinking. It gave her position and the fact that approximately 245 men were onboard and that two tugs were standing off to help when needed. It requested the assistance of any vessels in the vicinity. No Mayday, the international signal of a vessel in distress, was ever received by the U.S. Coast Guard or other authorities. The radio operators had just sent this message when suddenly their transmitters went dead: the water level had finally reached the generators, and immediately there was no more power. Radios, pumps, and all but emergency lighting went out. The shorting of the generators had also started a fire in the generator room. A cloud of smoke along with bluish and bright-green flames poured out of the generator-room ventilators.

Those on deck heard popping, like firecrackers going off, from the shorted generators. Then, in place of the omnipresent generator hum that had been their companion for every waking hour on the 269 and in place of the constant roar of the pump motors—there was silence. All the men now knew they were going down.

The crew of the *Captain John* had watched intently as the 269 lost her last towline, her bow anchors, and then her stern anchors. With the barge's stern settling into the sea, waves were breaking on top of her with devastating effect. Sometimes a wave loomed over her, then crashed not just on the afterdeck, which was all but submerged, but over the top of the tower, which was nearly 30 feet above deck. The tower, along with the entire aft end of the barge, was getting smashed with regularity.

Robert Trosclair watched the disaster unfold from his position at the helm of the tug. At this point he gave the conn to his first mate while he talked to Chuck Denning in Morgan City. With the loss of power on the 269, the *Captain John* and the *North Carolina* were the only means of communication, although Richard Lobb could still talk to the tugs with a hand-held radio. Robert told his boss that they had better find as much help as they could, because in his opinion the 269 was on her way down.

Before, the barge had merely been wounded. Now she was going through her death agonies. Seawater poured down the ladders from the main deck to the living quarters as waves swept across her. The last men known to be below, those who had been tending the pumps, the radio operators, and a few foremen, dragged themselves up the ladders to the main deck as water began funneling down on top of them. No sooner had these men appeared on deck than the 269, with a mighty shudder, rolled to starboard. Perhaps a hole had opened in her side where the anchor had previously pierced her or maybe a ballast tank had burst, but whatever the cause, with her lee rail nearly in the water, all the tanks, buoys, chambers, and cylinders that had been sloshing around crashed into the rail and, taking it with them, were lost in the sea.

After their work on deck was halted, the *maniobristas* had huddled together next to the small crane. Luis Domingo had made the beginner's mistake of lingering close to the foreman, who was talking on his walkie-talkie. When the foreman finished, he looked up, and the first man he saw was Luis. "You, you, you, and you," he said to Luis and three other nearby deckhands, "go below and go into every room and make sure no one is still below. Tell anyone you see to get up on deck—immediately!"

Why him? Again Luis had been given a suicide job. He and the other three crewmen went racing below, two heading forward and two aft, screaming for everyone to get on deck. Luis and one other man each took one of the long corridors running toward the bow. Luis's was on the port, or high, side, so it was relatively easy going with little water to wade through, although more kept pouring in as each wave rolled across the deck. There was almost no light except for the dim red emergency lights and the occasional glare coming from a momentarily opened stairwell leading topside.

Nevertheless, Luis obeyed orders, though he certainly didn't look carefully into each bunk room as he went running through the empty hall yelling that the piece of shit was sinking. In less than twenty minutes the four of them were back on deck and reported that they had seen no one below. With 245 men sheltering in every nook and cranny on deck and in the various offices, workrooms, and storage cubicles above deck, no one could do an accurate head count. Still, it was believed that everyone had gotten out of the two lower decks. Whether everyone would leave the barge in one piece was another question.

Lee Lloyd and those on the heliodeck who could see aft watched in horror as waves tore off the 20-foot-high, 18-foot-wide, ½-inch-thick steel door used as a weather protector to safeguard the vulnerable sat chamber and the gas shack that stood on top of it. The door was so immense that, like an airplane hangar door, it had to be raised and lowered hydraulically. Only lowered maybe once every few years in the worst weather, it had previously been lowered and locked in place. Now, after being torn off like a piece of cardboard, the 10-ton door simply flipped into the pipe alley with an explosion so loud it could be heard all over the 269, even above the roar of wind and waves. Further forward, welded to the deck on one side and to a deckhouse on the other, was a skid to which 3-foot-wide, 30-foot-long cylinders of helium were fastened. Each filled cylinder, under 3,000 pounds per square inch of pressure, was like a cocked bomb. As waves continued smashing across the deck, one of the cylinders broke loose and somehow was punctured. The initial explosion, according to witnesses, was exactly like a bomb going off. Then with a piercing shriek that deafened those nearby, the cylinder blasted diagonally off the skid and out to sea. Miraculously it neither set off the other helium cylinders nor killed anyone on its short, unguided journey.

Chuck Denning is laconic. The North Bank manager is definitely not prone to nervousness, yet that Sunday afternoon and evening he sat in North Bank's Morgan City office glued to the single-sideband receiver with white knuckles around his microphone for hours on end. Once the 269 lost power and could no longer transmit, the *Captain John* and Chuck were the primary remaining means of communication. The *North Carolina* could and did transmit, but since it was chartered by North Bank Towing, its captain, Richard Cassel, thought it proper for his friend Robert on the *Captain John* to be the primary conduit to Robert's own company.

Usually single-sideband frequencies, except for 2182 kHz, the international distress channel, are filled with a jumble of ship-to-ship and ship-to-shore communication. But on that Sunday afternoon 8 MHz, the channel that the *Captain John* and North Bank were using, was strangely quiet. Chuck Denning later reflected on the situation. "There's a lot of people on those megs, and generally you have a lot of trouble understanding your boats, 'cause everybody out there wants to talk. It's just a free high-frequency channel for hundreds of boats out there. But I think everybody tuned in to what was happening, you know. We had some vessels in distress, we had a barge sinking—and that radio was the quietest I've ever heard it. There was one boat that came on and someone was trying to talk. I advised them. I said, 'This is KZJ930, North Bank base in Morgan City. We have a vessel in distress, a barge sinking, and we'd appreciate you switching to another channel. We want to coordinate rescue efforts on this channel.' And they said, 'Roger,

Roger, Captain. Sorry,' you know, and they switched to another channel."

As the afternoon wore on, Robert filled in his boss as best he could on what was happening. Communication from the barge was sporadic. Chuck recalls: "Robert had gone through the whole scenario about how many times they'd parted towlines, that they were out of towlines, how everything was broke. I remember him telling me that the barge had dropped their anchors but they didn't appear to be holding. Right, first off, though, I got their latitude and longitude so we could pass their position on."

The *Captain John* had already given its position to the U.S. Coast Guard, as had the barge to its office in Carmen, from whom it requested assistance. But whether there would be *any* assistance available was unclear. There were other vessels in trouble and almost no ship large enough to brave the hurricane without itself becoming a victim. Although Mexico has no coast guard, it does have a navy, and modern patrol vessels were as close as the harbor at Carmen. However, the Mexican Navy reported to C.C.C. and to the 269 that their units could not leave port because of the tidal surge in the channel leading from the harbor to the Gulf. This seems odd, since the tidal surge would *increase,* not decrease, the water's depth in the channel. There may have been other factors in the Mexican Navy's decision. In any case, the Mexican Navy did nothing whatever. Nor were there any U.S. Coast Guard vessels closer than Key West, more than 650 miles away, and the seas being what they were, it might be two days before a Coast Guard ship could be on the scene. The rescue possibilities didn't look good. Fortunately, most men were unaware that virtually no help was available.

Shortly after 1600 the *Ducker Tide* finally appeared. The only boat that had answered their calls for help looked like she might not reach them. Smashing through waves and pitching over them, then plowing into the troughs until her pilothouse was covered in spray, it seemed as though she herself might go down. A handful of men in the tower and all those congregated on the walkway watched her arrive. Over his hand-held VHF, Richard Lobb advised her captain, "It doesn't look good. It looks like we have to get out." This was Lobb's last radio transmission. He and a small contingent of foremen and assistants pushed their way through the group of men on the walkway. The 269 was leaning far to starboard, and the tower could be buried under the barge should she capsize. What was now high above the deck could suddenly be far below the deck.

Others left the tower as well. Only Steve, Rozy, and Kevin remained. They watched the men on the tower walkway follow the superintendent's group toward the bow. The three men listened as one by one the captains of the tug and the two supply boats called in, requesting directions from Lobb. "Where do you want me?" one captain called. "Where do you need us?" another asked. Neither Lobb nor anyone from the barge responded. The calling went on with no answer. Finally, Kevin over his hand-held called Lobb. "Richard, where do you want the boats? I need to know where you want the boats. The boats are callin' in, can't you hear 'em?" Lobb never replied. On deck in the howling wind he wasn't able to hear anything. Kevin watched him throw his radio overboard.

Finally Kevin himself responded to the boats, telling them to stay downwind, that this was where the men would drift. Of course the captains already realized it, and two had positioned their vessels to the southeast of the barge. There were so many men in the water now that the captains were afraid to close with the sinking 269. In waters so filled with swimmers it would be all too easy to suck men in their props while they were attempting to rescue others.

At 1640 hours the leaden skies already made it seem like dusk. Sunset was only an hour off, and near the equator darkness soon follows. The stern of the 269 was sinking quickly, and her bow was pointing more and more like a diagonal arrow toward the hidden stars. Richard Lobb had made the decision. While there was some light left for the two tugs to see men in the water, they must abandon ship. On the *Captain John*, Robert Trosclair was talking to Chuck Denning. The captain paused in his transmission. When he came back on, he said, "Chuck, I have to break with you now. They advised me that they're fixing to abandon the barge. It's sinking. They asked me to stand by to start picking up people. Do you copy? Over." "Roger, Roger, I read you fine, Robert. I'll stay in the office and be here if you need me or if anything needs to be relayed to anybody. Good luck, Robert! KZJ930, Morgan City base with the *Captain John*, Whiskey-Charley-Yankee 5568—clear."

Robert's final comment was "Chuck, I don't know how it's all gonna come out and if I'm going to be able to rescue those people, but I'm sure going to give it a try. *Captain John*, Whiskey-Charley-Yankee 5568 to Morgan City base—clear."

Chuck looked at the microphone in his hand and wondered: With over 200 people in the water, with 80- or 90-mile-an-hour winds and with 35- or 40-foot seas, how in the hell are those boats going to rescue those people? He might have added: How in the hell are those captains going to keep their boats from rolling over while they're trying to rescue those people?

On the 269's bow Richard Lobb was going around telling everyone to get ready. "Shortly, guys, looks like we're gonna have to ditch." He walked up to a group of the dive crew and shook their hands. "Good luck," he told them. "Hope to see you on the other side when we get out of this."

Some men who had already jumped over the side were bobbing next to the barge. Most of them struggled to paddle clear of the 269 and to reach various rafts that had not been blown away by the wind. The public address system was no longer working, but it didn't matter. Word spread around the barge in a matter of minutes. It was time to go; the 269 was sinking. The moment that most of the men had been dreading all day, especially those who couldn't swim, had arrived. Those who were not already near the bow moved toward it. Dodging waves that were now sweeping regularly across the deck, timing their movements between one wave and the next, and struggling to climb the ever-more-tilting deck, the men scuttled forward. The men who were still on the heliodeck found that the water level had risen up the forward ladder that led to the main deck. Quickly they jumped down and waded toward the bow before splitting up, some heading toward the lower, starboard side and others to the mass of men gathered on the high, port side.

Many men had been at their life-raft stations all day, in some cases hugging their life-raft canisters, both to ensure themselves a place on the raft when it eventually deployed and to keep from getting washed over the side. More than once a huge sea had hit an exposed station, ripping the raft capsule from their arms and heaving it over the side, where immediately it inflated and, breaking its painter, was swept away. The crewmen were left holding empty capsule frames, and gradually they, too, staggered forward in a daze. Some men seemed shell-shocked, hollow, unable to comprehend their predicament. Others were screaming, often in Spanish, or praying. More men began leaping into the sea. Many of the Mexicans first crossed themselves, their mouths moving in prayer as they jumped. Some were being swept under the hull of the barge. With each wave more helpless men slammed into the hull or, worse, were lost beneath it.

One of the men watching the disintegration of the 269 was Victor Diaz. Victor could have passed for a Hollywood leading man. Tall and dark, with a broad, friendly grin, he was as intelligent as he was handsome. He and Rick Harris were the two lead dive tenders on the 269. They were in charge of all the divers' equipment and made sure everything functioned and was in place to be used at a moment's notice. Victor had graduated from California's College of Oceaneering in 1992, and since then had been working for McDermott on the 269 and other barges in the Gulf. Now he, Rick, and Danny Weidenboener, along with fifteen or twenty other men, were perched on top of a small house on the bow where one of the drums of anchor cable was kept.

Victor and the others looked out on a scene of total chaos. Behind them the deck ran downhill at a 45° angle. As he watched, one of the helium tanks that had broken loose hit something solid and exploded. The tracked Manitowac crane had been anchored to the deck with heavy chains. It had broken its shackles and was whipping back and forth around the deck like a giant toy. Waves were sweeping over most of the 269, with the only oasis above the sea being the corner of the bow on which many of the crew still congregated. Victor and most of the men on the cable house realized it was time to leave their perch. They made their way to the rail through screaming, panic-stricken men.

Victor described his last minutes onboard: "There were two men who were next to me and they were nationals and they were talking in Spanish to each other that in case one of them did not make it, to make sure he would tell his family that he loved them and it would go likewise. At the time this thing [the 269] was almost vertical, and it was extremely dark and the waves are really pounding. I looked at Rick Harris and I said, 'Hey, bud, I'll buy you a cold one if we survive this.'

"I was trying to make my way through the crowd, and all the men, like they didn't want to move, they didn't want to budge. It took a great deal of strength for me to shove a few of them out of the way so I could jump into the water. But before I'd done that I could see the waves as they passed between each crest and the valley, and the way the barge was—it was a heck of a drop, a heck of a drop. Everybody was so freakin' terrified that nobody wanted to jump. As I jumped into the water I was making sure that I didn't land on top of anybody. One of the biggest and the worst things from this whole event is the constant roar of the waves as they passed by. It sounded like—you ever been by the side of the road and you hear an eighteen-wheeler pass by you? That's how loud it was."

As the men prepared to jump into the hurricane-driven seas, their last thoughts before they leaped became imprinted in their memories. Shane Richins's little boy was celebrating his fourth birthday that Sunday, and Shane wondered if that date would also be the anniversary of his father's death. Just before jumping, Lenn Cobb looked at his watch. "We got an hour of daylight," he said to himself. "If 50 percent [of the men] make it, it'll be a miracle." Rob Whaley was pissed because they all were going to miss the Sunday steak barbecue.

Few men say they took their predicament as lightly as Rob did. Raul Salabania Acosta, the young valve technician, stood by the starboard rail, now nearly underwater. While others were leaping into the sea, he was transfixed. He saw himself in his coffin. His soul hovered over his corpse, looking down on it, crying. Raul agonized, praying and crying beneath the vision of his soul.

For the last few weeks Raul had worried constantly about the 269's sinking. During Hurricane Opal, two weeks before Roxanne hit, he thought the old tub would go down. With the little transistor radio he carried, he always listened to the weather reports, and as Roxanne came closer he spent much of his free time near the radio room, where he could learn the most, picking up bits of information and the never-ending rumors about how the bosses planned to dodge the hurricane.

Earlier that day all the bosses had been in the radio room. He overheard them discussing how to stop the leaks coming up through the floor of the recreation room. The bosses, seeing Raul and a few others eavesdropping, told them to go up on deck.

Raul huddled with a couple of other guys in a store-room on deck and continued worrying. He thought about Bruna at home with their five children. Who would care for them if he died? They had been married twenty years, since he was eighteen. She had always worried that he would be in an accident at sea and urged him to try to get a job ashore. Now, maybe her prophecy was coming true. The captain passed by their storeroom and Raul asked him, "What do we gotta do?" The captain answered, "Wait. Don't do anything."

So Raul waited, along with all the others. He was amidships, by the rail on the starboard side. As the 269 settled in the sea the water came closer and closer. The water came right up to him, to his legs, and he retreated higher on the deck, but he could hardly move. He started to feel like he was already dead. And in his mind all he could see was his dead body in the coffin. His weeping soul still hovered over his corpse. Raul agonized, praying and crying with his soul. Finally, realizing that he had no choice, he dropped into the sea. He went under and immediately was swept down and forward of the 269's bow. When he surfaced, there was only the sea around him. In spite of the raging waves he suddenly felt different, assured—almost as though a load had been lifted from his shoulders. He knew he would survive.

As Lee Lloyd left the heliodeck, he kept repeating to himself that he was going to do everything he could to be vigilant and to keep his wits about him at every moment to make sure he got home. He would get home to see his family once more, no matter what happened. A southern Baptist living in southern Louisiana where everyone, including his family, was Catholic, Lee attended mass every Sunday, even though he had never converted. During the course of that Sunday he found himself saying a number of Hail Marys. He found himself repeating "Pray for us sinners now and at the hour of our death. Amen," and it took on a new meaning for him.

Lee watched Tim Noble and some others head toward their life-raft station two-thirds of the way up the starboard side. The 269 was leaning more and more to starboard. Waves sweeping along it had carried away all the starboard inflated rafts, and a strong current also appeared to be flowing underneath the barge from that side. Lee saw some of his fellow shipmates preparing to jump the few feet into the water there, but he turned away. Lee still feared the 269 would roll over, trapping beneath her all those in the water on the starboard side. So he moved forward and joined the mass of men on the port bow, which by this time jutted nearly 40 feet above the water.

Some of the men congregated on the bow were

screaming or wailing, but most waited, silently watching the fate of those who had already jumped and who
were struggling in the water below. Those in the water
tried to avoid being hit by men jumping on top of
them, to avoid the flotsam that littered the water, and
to get away from the steel hulk that would surely
carry them down with it when it sank. And finally, the
swimmers desperately struck out toward the nearest
rafts, perhaps their only means of salvation.

Shane Richins and Clay Horschel joined Lee.
The three divers, the only three left who had worked
together for McDermott's diving division before it
merged with Offshore Pipelines, made a pact to stick
together no matter what. Ray Pepperday, Mitch Pheffer, and Phil Richard also were there, looking down as-
sessing the situation and waiting for the best moment
to jump.

Danny Weidenboener, a dive tender, had joined
them, looking like an explorer headed for the jungle.
Prepared for any eventuality, Danny was festooned
with knives, ropes, rolls of duct tape, and a water jug,
all hanging from a dive belt. Those around him wondered if he would float.

Whereas, minutes before, few men had wanted
to go over the side, suddenly it seemed that everyone
was leaving the sinking ship at once. Men were jumping pell-mell on top of one another, or just missing

those already in the water. Clay, Shane, and Lee threw two life rafts into the water, and men, seeing the rafts hit, leaped onto the tops of the deployed rafts, crushing those who had just climbed inside. But usually, as soon as most rafts hit the water and inflated, they were gone before the jumpers could reach them, blown away by the screaming wind.

While some of the dive crew waited for an open space into which they could jump, Jim Vines came up to them. Jim was one of the barge foremen. In his late forties, he was heavy and not in the best physical condition. With pleading eyes, he said, "Look, you guys. I don't know how to swim very well. Can I go with you? Will you all look out for me and help me?"

By this time the divers were climbing over the railing, getting ready to jump. Shane assured him, "Yeah, Jim. Just follow us. We're all gonna go together and you can just go with us and we'll grab one those life rafts."

One raft still attached by its painter to the barge floated a few hundred feet to leeward. Lee turned to Vines: "OK, Jim, all right, it's time to go," and Vines climbed nervously over the rail alongside the divers who had agreed, "Everybody, OK, it's time to go." "Let's hit it! Oh shit . . ." "OK, Jim," Lee added, "we're all gonna go on three. One, two, three. . ." Lee jumped, then Clay, Lenn, Shane, Mitch, Phil, Ray

Pepperday, and finally Danny Weidenboener. After hitting the water, each man went under, then quickly bobbed back to the surface.

When Lee hit the water he looked up and saw Jim Vines climbing back across the rail onto the deck of the barge. Terrified, Vines couldn't bring himself to jump. But those in the sea could now do nothing to help him.

The 269, which had twice hit bottom within the last hour, suddenly hit bottom again. The few men still on the vessel were thrown to the deck. So were Steve Howell and Kevin in the tower. Rozy had just left but managed to wrap his arms around a stanchion supporting the tower railing to keep from being tossed overboard. A computer monitor broke loose and hit Kevin on the back of the head. A moment later, a wave bigger than those preceding it smashed in one of the tower's safety-glass windows, flooding the room.

Steve and Kevin got to their feet. Rozy was still wrapped around his stanchion. As Steve headed for the door, he yelled, "Kevin, let's get the fuck out of here!" Kevin, wobbly from the blow to his head, found himself alone. He focused on what he had to do to save himself. He knew he had to take off his heavy work boots, because they would weigh him down in the water. He still had his VHF and tried to call the

North Carolina to tell it to be off the starboard side.
Standing up, with water to his waist, Kevin waded
toward the door just as another wave hit. By this time
the tower was nearly at sea level, so as each wave
crashed into it, the door, which normally opened out
but now faced the incoming rollers, wouldn't open.
For a few terrifying moments Kevin felt trapped
inside. Between waves he finally managed to get the
door open. Steve was gone, but Rozy still waited for
him.

"Kevin," Rozy yelled, "you didn't take your boots
off!"

"Fuck my boots. Let's get outta here."

"No, Kevin, you gotta take 'em off. Come on,
take your boots off." The 6-foot-3-inch Rozy swept up
the 5-foot-8-inch Kevin like a grizzly bear and pinned
him against the railing until Kevin was able to yank
his boots off. They walked around to the front of the
tower. Waves roared by them and the following
troughs sank below them.

"You go first," Kevin yelled to Rozy.

"No, you go ahead. I'll be right behind you."

Kevin jumped and lost track of everything.

As dusk fell upon the hulk of the *269*, now
mostly underwater, almost everyone had abandoned
it. The heliodeck still remained above the waves,
which, unrestrained, swept over the remains of the

barge. On the heliodeck a small, lonely figure stood by itself. It looked like a part of the barge—a vertical fixture attached to the deck plates rather than anything resembling a living being. The figure neither moved nor called out nor even seemed to notice the devastation surrounding it or the seas that soon would envelop it. Luis Domingo appeared to be frozen in time and space, a little statue of flesh and bone.

That afternoon, as soon as he was free of the deck gang, Luis Domingo had joined others on the heliodeck. Already some of the crew who had been there most of the day began leaving. They worked their way forward to the crowded areas near the bow and eventually disappeared over one side or the other. A few called out to him to leave with them, but he could not. From his vantage point looking down over the main deck, Luis watched as more and more of his shipmates fled the 269. He wanted desperately to join them, but he was so afraid of being in those raging seas that he couldn't bring himself to move. He was physically frozen. His muscles wouldn't work, so he just watched the exodus until the last stragglers wrenched themselves from whatever they had been hanging on to and leaped overboard. Finally the 269's decks were bare except for the waves sweeping across them. The entire ship was empty except for him. This made his situation much worse. Now his fear was joined by three more Mexicans and by two other Americans, who hauled themselves over the side. When it appeared that their raft might get dragged down by the sinking barge, someone cut the tether. Immediately they took off, driven by the elements in a wild downwind rush. Their journey was a terrifying one.

Lenn and the other divers just shook their heads in disbelief. Never in their collective decades at sea had they seen anything like this. The waves were vertical walls of water 30 feet, sometimes 40 feet high, and unlike larger ocean swells that a vessel could slide over, these came only a few seconds apart and were so steep that it was impossible to ride them. Their puny raft would try to climb a wave, get halfway up, and then cave in, fold in half, throwing those on the high side on top of those below. Then the whole raft and its human cargo would plunge below the surface as if being driven by a locomotive, and down it would stay for two or three agonizing seconds. It would gradually emerge and begin its rapid ascent of the next wave, where again it would collapse and again be driven back into the trough. Hour after hour the process endlessly repeated itself. The men seemed to be below the surface more than they were above it. If they didn't hold their breaths at just the right moment, they would be choking on seawater

A monstrosity to take through a hurricane, *Derrick Lay Barge 264*
(*DLB-264*) is generally similar to *DLB-269*, which sank in
Hurricane Roxanne, except that the helicopter pad on
the *269* was just in front of the big crane.

COURTESY OF OFFSHORE PIPELINES INC.

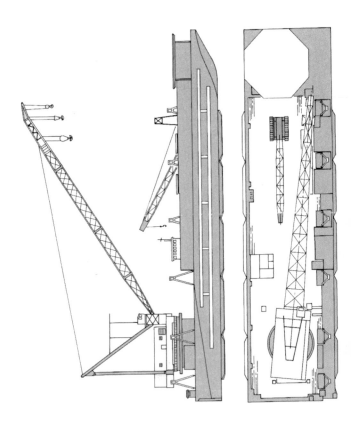

Simplified topside layout of *DLB-264*. The diagram from Offshore Pipelines Inc.'s spec sheet probably incorrectly shows the crane's A-frame not joined to the boom. The six davits on the starboard side are used to raise sections of pipe.

COURTESY OF OFFSHORE PIPELINES INC.

North Bank Towing's 110-foot tug, the *Captain John*, the smallest of
the three rescue vessels, whose crew pulled eighty-nine survivors
from the waves.

The *Seabulk North Carolina*. The third vessel, the *Ducker Tide*,
looks almost the same as the *North Carolina*.

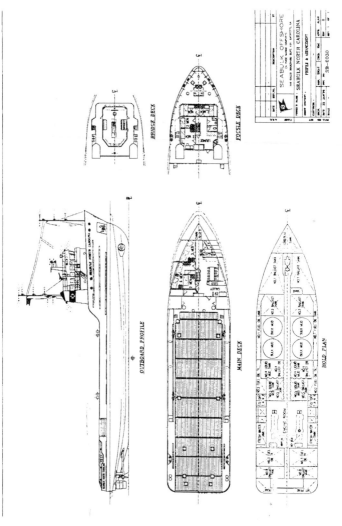

Diagrams of the supply boat *Seabulk North Carolina*,
one of only three vessels to attempt to
rescue 230 men in the sea.

The dive crew shortly after the rescue and before their departure from Ciudad del Carmen. Left to right, standing: Roy Cline, Lee Lloyd, Clay Horschel, Shane Richins, O.P. Chauvin, Ray Pepperday, Victor Diaz, Ricky Perez, Mitch Pheffer, Chuck Rountree, Tim Noble, John Wheeler, Lenn Cobb, Rob Whaley; kneeling: Kris Nielson, Phil Richard, Rob Boettger, Rick Harris. Missing from this group picture are Ron Rozmarynoski (inset), whose broken leg was being treated, and Danny Weidenboener.

Captain Robert Trosclair almost lost his life during the rescue. He received an award from U.S. Coast Guard Admiral Robert North, commander, 8th Coast Guard District. At left is Chuck Denning. The captains and all the crew members of the three rescuing vessels received awards.

Only Captain Harold Roche and his crew on the *Ducker Tide* were brave enough to sail into the hurricane in response to the distress calls from the 269 and her tugs.

COURTESY OF TANYA ROCHE TRAHAN

Luis Domingo de la Riva thought for sure he would die aboard the sinking 269.

COURTESY OF M. KRIEGER

Raul Salabania Acosta, terrified, was transfixed by the vision of his corpse hovering over him.

COURTESY OF M. KRIEGER

Eulalio Zapata, first mate of the *North Carolina*, risked his life time and time again. By himself, he pulled dozens of men from the sea.

Kevin Dumont predicted disaster and urged his superiors to have the *269* towed to safety. Unfortunately no one in authority listened to him.

Lorenzo Wilson, first mate of the *Captain John*, and his men were nearly swept off of their tug's deck during the rescue.

Roberto Cruz Gomez, "El Padre," lost his life during the rescue.

A Clyde 60DE revolving crane, similar to the one on the 269.

COURTESY OF O.P.I. BROCHURE

The diving bell on the 269 could have been the coffin for the six divers going through decompression.

COURTESY OF T. NOBLE

and gasping for air as they tried to prepare for the next onslaught—only seconds away.

Everyone became exhausted trying to hang on as the raft continued to cave in. They found it nearly impossible to withstand the force of the waves. Before each collapse of their raft they tried to fend each other off a bit or to blunt the inevitable collisions of one man into another so that they didn't smash heads or break limbs. But that was all they could do, except for trying to sweep out the seawater that nearly filled the raft by using their arms as paddles. That, too, was useless. Early on they had lost sight of the 269 as well as the other rafts and the rescue vessels. Now it was getting dark and they began to fear that they would not be rescued. They felt completely alone until a most unexpected visitor appeared.

As the despairing men began their ascent of a particularly large wave, Lenn glanced up toward the wave's peak. There, surfing on the crest as easily as a bird flying through the air—and staring down at them—was a full-grown dolphin. Their eye contact lasted only a few seconds before the raft collapsed in the wave and they were again buried beneath the surface.

On the roller-coaster ride up the next crest, he looked up to see two dolphins high above the raft intently watching them. The dolphins seemed to be smiling. They were obviously curious, not threatening in any way, and so much at home in the crashing waves, so adept at navigating the tempest, that he and the few others who could see the dolphins felt intensely envious of them.

On each succeeding wave at least one dolphin and sometimes three or four effortlessly surged above them. In each instance the men and the dolphins looked directly at each other. And what did the dolphins think? Could they read the fear in the men's eyes? Who knows? In any case, after a few minutes they disappeared, and once more the men in the raft were alone in the towering seas.

Not all the crew were able to get to rafts so easily. Ray Pepperday, the young sat technician, remembers jumping and hitting the water so hard he felt like he got a saltwater enema. Perhaps his life preserver was one with poor flotation, because he seemed to go far under and then wasn't able to get back to the surface. He began to swim underwater, trying to reach the surface, but, disoriented, he couldn't determine which way was up. Finally he realized he would have to depend on whatever flotation existed in his preserver to save him. Slowly he rose, hoping he would reach the surface before he had to take a breath.

Ray broke water gasping. He emerged almost under the barge and could feel a current pulling at him, sucking him back beneath the barnacle-covered hull. In desperation he pushed off with his feet and tried to swim away. After about five minutes of furious breast stroking, Ray found that he was getting nowhere. He just couldn't seem to get away from it. Finally, alternately side stroking and swimming on his back, he started to put some distance between himself and the barge.

Exhausted, Pepperday stopped to look back at the 269. It was almost vertical in the water, the bow sticking nearly straight up. In amazement he watched a Mexican crewman scaling a rope, like climbing up a 120-foot cliff, for some reason trying to get back on deck, or what was left of it.

He also looked around for the young divers, Phil Richard and Mitch Pheffer. They had found a raft that somehow had been trapped in a calm spot and hadn't been blown away. Ray saw it and began swimming toward them, but he was so tired that it was slow going. And when he finally reached the raft, he had no energy to pull himself out of the water. So he just hung alongside for a while trying to regain some strength.

Using the lines running along the perimeter of the raft, and with a little help from those inside, Ray was soon able to hoist himself aboard. Mitch and Phil were already in the raft along with Chuck Rountree and four or five of the Mexican crew. The 10-foot-diameter raft, meant to hold fifteen people, was still not crowded. However, being one of the closest rafts to the barge, it soon filled with weary, frightened men. Within twenty minutes of the time Pepperday climbed in, the raft was bulging with twenty-five or thirty people all fighting for space.

By this time the overloaded raft had drifted out from the lee of the barge and was back in the maelstrom, no longer floating much above the sea. It would ride up a big wave crest, but before reaching the top it would fall off and the wave would crash on top of it, burying it in the sea. Three or four men who were hanging on the outside would get swept away and would have to paddle madly to regain the raft. The only saving grace was that the center of gravity was so low that wave after crushing wave couldn't turn it over.

This raft, like all the others that had landed upside down, couldn't be righted easily, since its floor had become its top. And the slippery canopy, now the floor, sagged alarmingly with all the bodies kneeling in the middle. Those in the center had no lines to hold on to, nothing except each other. They jostled for space, fighting to keep their heads above the deep pool that had collected under them.

Rountree, the diving supervisor, was one of

those in the center. A tall, blond athlete, Chuck was in reasonably good shape. Still, he was in his fifties, and during the ordeal, which had worn him down, he had injured his foot. He struggled to keep his head above water, but those he was pushing against were frantic and less than half his age. He started getting shoved beneath other men. Alarmed, Ray, Mitch, and Phil pulled him up between them to a spot along the raft's inner periphery, where he hung from a lifeline gasping for air.

As time passed, the four divers became worried that those in the center would drown. They tried to convey to their Mexican comrades that the raft was upside down and that they all needed to climb out so that they could right it. But none of the divers could speak enough Spanish to make themselves understood. The Mexicans, many terrified and nearly all suspicious, were not going back into the sea for anything. Knives appeared, and the attempt to right the raft was abandoned. So they drifted. On top of wave crests they would catch glimpses of the *Captain John*, the *Carolina*, and another boat, but since none of the rescuing craft came anywhere near them or seemed to see them, they just hung on.

Rescuing men in such circumstances was all but absurd. The rescuers faced the real possibility that their boats might go broadside to the seas and capsize while bringing men onboard. The smaller *Captain John* didn't roll as badly as the two supply boats, but her afterdeck was lower, barely 5 feet above the water, and breaking waves were sweeping it with a vengeance. Tons of white water surged over the deck, engulfing everything on it. How could any man stand up to that deluge? The waves came so fast that the men would have only a second or two to save themselves.

As they waited for Robert Trosclair to guide the tug into position for their attempt to bring aboard the first swimmers, Lorenzo Wilson, the tall, angular Nicaraguan first mate, and the four crew members huddled in the shelter of the big winch drum just aft of the deckhouse. Pedro, Vincent, Wilbert, and Victor Vega, the engineer, looked apprehensively as a wave swept the deck on which they would be working.

"I'm just as scared as you," Lorenzo told them. "We might get washed overboard or this boat might go down, but we aren't gonna worry about that right now. What we gonna do," he continued, fingering a coil of ⅜-inch nylon line, "is use this so we don't get washed over the side."

The men cut 20-foot lengths, fastened the ends around themselves, and tied off the other ends on deck gear. They had brought all the tug's life rings aft, and as the *Captain John* came up to the first group of half a dozen swimmers, they tied the line ends of the preservers to cleats under the bulwarks and tossed the rings to the men in the water. Then two men together would pull a swimmer in over the rail. They were able to get the men on deck, but the safety-line experiment was a disaster. By the time they got the first few men onboard the five rescuers were so tangled in each other's safety lines that they could hardly move. They looked at each other in exasperation. Now what?

Lorenzo called his men together. "All right, we gotta take off our lines." Wilbert, the oldest of the deckhands, shook his head. "Come on, Wilbert, take off your line. Nobody gonna be tied. Just be sure that when a wave is coming you pick something to hold on to. All right?" Lorenzo continued looking at his reluctant crew. "I gotta protect you and you gotta protect me. If a wave is coming, you warn the other guys. You hold on and help the guy next to you."

Each time a wave was about to hit, someone would yell out. They dropped to their knees and grabbed the bulwark supports welded to the deck. The waves crashed over them, covering them with white water. In seconds the sea drained out the tug's scuppers and they would get up and again begin pulling people in.

One wave, however, came unnoticed until the last instant. The men turned to see the enormous breaker just before it crashed over the stern. Victor grabbed a support, Lorenzo, one of the bitts, and the others, all except Pedro, at gear next to them. Pedro was caught flat-footed. The wave carried him across the deck, first throwing him against the deckhouse, then into the starboard bulwarks, and finally, all within two or three seconds, it began to wash him back over the stern. Fortunately he grabbed an 8-inch pipe that supported the towing cable tie-down and kept himself from being carried overboard. Afterward he could hardly get up. He thought every bone in his body was broken, though in fact he had suffered no broken bones. Somehow he continued working.

Raul Acosta, the valve technician who had seen his soul crying over his corpse, was fortunate. Not long after he jumped into the sea, a raft floated nearby still attached to the barge. Raul swam to it, and the single occupant, a young Mexican he didn't know, pulled him in. Once in the raft he took stock of the situation. Their raft had a half-dozen lines, mostly tangled and all leading back to the barge. Each time the 269 rolled or pitched over a wave, their raft followed it with a sickening lurch. Back and forth they went. More sodden men began climbing into the raft until it became crowded. The men already inside looked apprehensive as each newcomer clambered in. Finally two men began cutting the lines holding them. As they were cutting the last line, Miguel Alvarez Cantu, the acting captain, paddled up looking like a drowned rat. He no longer had the 269's registration, log, and crew manifest. The men dragged him in and he flopped among all the ordinary crewmen. An old American guy was also pulled in.

As soon as the last tether was cut, the overflowing raft headed downwind, more in the water than out of it. The occupants wondered how long the bulging raft would be able to withstand the waves that were heaving it skyward and then burying it in their troughs. Everybody inside, besides hanging on to each other, seemed to be praying.

Maybe their prayers were answered. After about an hour the pitching raft was spotted by Trosclair. As the tug came alongside, he took his engines out of gear. One after another all the men in the raft were grabbed by the *Captain John's* crew and pulled onboard. Raul Acosta got to his feet on the tug's deck and hurried below, away from the maelstrom. However, his ordeal was not over.

Marco Polo Ramirez, the diver, had to push his buddy Diego off the barge before he could jump. Diego couldn't swim, and even with his friend's assurance that he would stay with him and help him, the man refused to budge. Finally Marco threw Diego in and then jumped himself at a point on the starboard side that was only 10 feet above the water. Marco had his eye on an empty raft, still tethered to the barge, that bobbed close by, probably less than 100 feet away. He could certainly pull Diego that far. Once they were in the water, Marco struck out for the raft, Diego in tow. With his strong swimmer's stroke, and even getting his friend to kick a little, they were able to reach the raft without much trouble. The instant they pulled themselves over the side, however, they heard a hiss of air and the raft collapsed around them. No wonder there was no one in it. Some rafts had been torn on deck gear even before they were in the water. Some snagged on flotsam in the sea. But the majority of leaky rafts had succumbed to swimmers scrambling in who were still wearing their steel-cleated work boots.

Once more the two men were in the water. Diego wanted to go back to the barge. Marco Polo tried to reason with him. They didn't want to be anywhere near it. With waves breaking over them it was impossible to talk to his friend. Anyway, it didn't make any difference. Diego was incapable of propelling them in any direction. The only trouble was that Marco could no longer tow him against the current, which was now sweeping them back toward the barge. Soon they found themselves being driven under the great dark bow. Even though the 269 was half submerged, each wave lifted the bow and then slammed it back into the next trough. The two men were sucked under the hull as if by a giant vacuum.

Floating under the 269 was like being in a roaring underwater room whose ceiling kept descending on them. The hull seemed to be smashing down harder and harder. Each time it came down it propelled the swimmers farther underwater, tearing them on its barnacles.

Marco panicked. He had lost control. He was pulled farther under the barge and could not get out from under it. By this time he was totally underwater. With his last lungful of air he swam desperately to escape. He never even felt the barnacles ripping his skin from head to toe. After what seemed like hours he drifted clear of the barge, and this time the current propelled him away from the 269. Marco looked all around for his friend without seeing him. Diego, whom he had lost under the hull, certainly was dead. Unable to save his friend, Marco realized he now had to focus on saving himself.

He began swimming first on his stomach, then on his back. He dodged debris and swallowed some oil, which made him retch. While swimming on his back, he bumped into something soft. He turned over to see another fellow he knew from the crew. Together they half-drifted and half-swam until they spotted two men in a raft. The guys helped pull them inside, where they collapsed. Gradually other swimmers struggled up to the raft and were helped aboard. Eventually there were nine of them.

Water kept filling the raft. The men tore off their shoes and tried unsuccessfully to sweep it out. Hours passed without seeing anyone. Eventually someone yelled that he saw a rescue boat. Maybe he did and maybe he didn't. Perhaps it was just spindrift blowing in the wind. Suddenly, right in front of them, a ship broke through a wall of spray. It was so big it filled their entire horizon.

Before the men in the raft even had time to become scared, the *Ducker Tide* was between them and the waves, drifting down toward them. Lines were thrown to them by crewmen at a break in the bulwarks amidships. The raft was pulled next to the hull, and at this point the men inside became frightened, because the *Ducker* rose above them on each crest and smashed down next to them in each trough, throwing a wave that threatened to overturn their little raft. Three of the men in the raft grabbed life rings thrown to them and were pulled onboard. The rest could only watch terrified as the *Ducker Tide* rose, then crashed back down a few feet from killing them. Their eyes were riveted on a single man who leaned over the break in the bulwarks. Each time the *Ducker* rolled off a wave, his arm snaked out and grabbed the nearest guy in the raft and in one motion flung him on deck. The arm that grabbed on to each belt or life preserver was like a steel spring. It was the size of most men's thighs, and it yanked one after another of the soaked, helpless men onboard until the raft was nearly empty.

The last man in Marco's raft even Hayman Webster could not deal with alone. Tinto was not just fat, he was huge. He had nearly not been hired because of his weight, but he was a fine welder and his skills were much in demand. It had taken five men just to pull Tinto into the raft, and when the mate saw him he looked like a small whale alongside the *Ducker*. Webster knew he would need help. Two others on deck joined him. They got Tinto to tie a line under his arms, and together, grunting and heaving, sliding and falling on the slippery, pitching deck, somehow they were able to get him aboard. Afterward his rescuers glanced at each other in amazement, smiling at what they had just accomplished. But a looming wave quickly ended their momentary celebration, and they dove for cover.

Hayman Webster, the first mate of the *Ducker*,

is not a man to be fooled with. The son of a Nicaraguan seafarer, he is generally taciturn and is not everyone's best friend. But he sees that his ship is well run and that everyone does his job—and no one complains, at least to his face, for Hayman is 6 feet 2 inches and 220 pounds of solid muscle. Many of the first thirty men hauled onboard his vessel had him to thank for saving their lives. He did it with a shrug. It was part of the job.

Before Tim Noble left the 269, he walked around the bow looking for the best place to jump. The port bow was sticking 40 feet above the water. So he headed back along the port side to find a lower spot. He and Rob Boettger had decided to go together. But when Tim reached the place about 60 feet from the bow where he had left Boettger standing by the rail, all that was left was Rob's boots. Kris Nielsen, Rob Whaley, and a few others were still there preparing to jump and head for a raft that tied off opposite them. They went, and Tim was about to follow when he saw John Enriques, the 269's Spanish assistant captain, hanging from a painter directly below him. The barge would rise on a wave and Enriques would dangle in the air. Then the 269 would wallow in the next trough and Enriques would get sucked in under the hull, but he wouldn't let go of the line. Tim finally got John to release the line and jump. When Enriques hit the water, Tim followed him in, but before he leaped he looked for the raft. It was gone; someone had cut the painter.

As soon as Tim landed in the water, the current and wind swept him away from the 269. He said, "I took off. I was off to the races." In just a few minutes he and Enriques were carried so far that when they looked back toward the barge, it had disappeared.

Where many men were afraid of being in the sea, Tim was not. In fact, he was confident of his ability to survive in the hurricane's waves. He came from a long line of seafarers. His great-grandfather was a ship's captain, as were some of his uncles. For twenty years his father, Jim, had been a diver in the Navy. After that his father worked for Taylor Diving, the first worldwide diving company. Tim had taken dive training himself in the Navy in 1971 and had worked his way up to diving in the Navy's elite Auxiliary Submarine Rescue Unit. After the Navy, he dove in the North Sea for a McDermott-owned company. Then he was transferred to his present assignment as one of the two shift supervisors on the 269. At age forty-two he was in excellent physical condition.

Of all the men on the 269, Tim and the other divers were certainly the best prepared mentally and physically to survive in the water. Used to potentially dangerous situations, they were able to stay in control of themselves in hazardous circumstances. As Tim describes it, "Divers have a mentality that I would characterize as having a constant cross-check with themselves. If they are OK [physically], then everything is OK. You don't consider what can happen, because if you do you'll never get anything done."

So when Tim hit the water and saw no raft available, he wasn't particularly bothered. John Enriques was nervously trying to swim nearby. Tim floated alongside him, keeping eye contact and getting him to settle down and relax. The wind and current swiftly swept them eastward. After a while they were propelled over an especially large wave. When Tim surfaced after being buried in the next trough, he couldn't find John. Nor did searching the surrounding area as he was carried up on succeeding wave crests reveal any sign of the Spanish assistant captain. He cursed himself for losing the man who he knew needed his help.

Besides carrying two dive knives, Tim had equipped himself with a flashlight and a 100-foot ¼-inch line before going over the side of the 269. Eventually he drifted out of sight of the barge. When, later, he came across a small group of survivors, and remembering how quickly Enriques had vanished, he offered to use the line to tie himself to the other swimmers. Joining together would increase their chances of being seen and rescued, he thought. It could also help to save someone who otherwise might drown. Even the most inexperienced landlubber instinctively realized that being lashed together was a good idea. So as Tim found others bobbing in the waves, they were added to the little group.

Especially during the first hour they were afloat, the bound stragglers also contended with debris from the 269. These weren't tiny objects, but 55-gallon drums and half-filled grease buckets. When flotsam was driven off a crest, it came hurtling at the men as if it had been thrown off a cliff. Getting hit with a 10-gallon grease can could kill you. So when flotsam came rushing toward them, the men tried frantically to dodge it or fend it off.

Tim and his group had been in the water about two hours when O. P. Chauvin and three crewmen floated by, clinging to a bright orange Norwegian buoy and a big plank. Tim managed to work his way over to Chauvin and tie him onto the line. O. P. would later undergo more hardship than any other survivor of the 269. But now he just floated with the others, still holding tightly to the buoy. The fellow with the plank presented a special hazard. The young Mexican had been hit by a giant wave while still on the deck of the barge and the front of his life vest had been torn off.

When he leaped into the Gulf, he had almost no flotation, but he found a plank to cling to. The problem was that his plank was studded with nails. So Tim fastened him at the opposite end of the line and tried to stay as far away as possible.

Like the survivors in the rafts, the swimmers kept rising up on the great crests, then sliding down the waves' backs until they were covered in the troughs. Each time they headed down, the men held their breath, realizing they would momentarily be stuffed beneath the surface. Sometimes they went under for just a second or two. Other times they were shoved far underwater, and it felt like agonizing minutes, even though it might have been only three or four seconds, before their life jackets brought them back up.

They reached the surface coughing and vomiting, and then with the meager time allotted them, they sucked in air for the next wave burial. The experience of being on the top of a big wave and looking 40 feet down into the trench and knowing that in a few seconds you were going to be plunged into it was frightening, far worse than riding any engineered roller coaster. And with each near-drowning the men grew weaker.

As they rode up another roller, Tim saw one of the crew, a young Mexican welding inspector, maybe

50 feet in front of them. He was on his back, kicking furiously, looking neither right nor left but straight into the sky. Oblivious to everything around him, at the top of his lungs he screamed his wife's name. "Carmella, Carmella, Carmella," he pleaded to the heavens as he went passing by them at right angles. His body was later found floating in the sea.

Dusk turned into night. As the little group of men rose to the wave tops, they could see the lights of the rescue boats going back and forth, sometimes a half-mile from them, sometimes a mile or two. Tim aimed his flashlight at the closer boats as they went by, but no one saw them. It grew colder, and with their constant dunkings and the wind screeching over them, the swimmers began to lose heart. Even Tim, perhaps the most experienced diver on the 269, started to have doubts about their survival.

Chapter Seven

~

A FTER JUMPING OFF the 269, Lee Lloyd and the other dive-crew members swam to the two nearby rafts still tethered to the barge. Lee's raft was already packed with men, so he and Shane Richins simply hung onto the lines running around the raft's exterior and floated with it. Most of the two dozen men in the raft just sat or squatted or stared vacantly. Some were shivering even though the sea was near bath temperature. Not long after the divers reached the raft, someone cut the painter and they were swept away. In a few minutes they could hardly see the barge. Within fifteen minutes it had disappeared.

The waves looked far larger at water level than they had from the bow of the 269. In fact, they were immense, with breaking crests. Because Lee's raft was overloaded, it continually filled with seawater, though it never capsized. The men had been in the sea only about an hour and it was just getting dark when one of the rescue vessels approached them. Visibility was so bad—with blowing spume, rain, and a ceiling so low that the clouds seemed to be rising from the sea—that neither Lee nor the men in his raft were aware of the vessel until it was almost on top of them.

The bow of the *Ducker Tide* came smashing through the center of a wave like an express train crashing through the side of a building. It even sounded like a train. Some of the survivors compared it to the noise of a roaring locomotive combined with a screaming jet engine. Shane remembered seeing the *Ducker Tide* coming toward them. "The bow of that ship would go up on top of a wave, and it seemed like you were looking at the Empire State Building. And then he [the captain] was trying to get as close to us as he could, and the knife-edge of that bow, you know, just seemed like it was gonna come right down on top of us."

As the *Ducker* reached the raft, it was falling down a wave. Its bow just slid by the raft, but Lee, who was still in the water, had become separated from the others. He looked up to see the overwhelming keel of the *Ducker* descending on top of him. Instead of being hit by the keel, however, he was pushed by a wall of water ahead of the bow and driven into the depths. The water buffer, a liquid sledgehammer, pounded him into the sea, but it kept him from being crushed by the hull. For an eternity he tumbled underwater. He had no control of his movements, nor could he, nearly unconscious, formulate any plan to save himself. Like a rag doll he rolled and flopped, wondering if he would die.

When Lee finally broke the surface, sputtering and coughing, he was amidships, near where the boat deck angled down to the afterdeck. The *Ducker* was still pitching wildly. As another wave came, the bow climbed it and the 2-foot-diameter bow thruster in its transverse tunnel vibrated, making the entire forward section of the ship shudder uncontrollably. He could see half the vessel's keel, still nearly on top of him. Then the *Ducker* plunged into the following trough, and as the stern came out of the water, the two giant propellers, each larger than Lee's 6-foot frame, shrieked and the whole vessel shook as if it would break apart. Lee was deafened and he was terrified.

Watching the vessel pitch like a bathtub toy and feeling its roar and vibrations coursing through him, Lee wanted only to get as far away from it as he could. He tried feebly to signal it to go away and leave him alone in the sea, which by comparison now seemed comforting. Then the door of the wheelhouse opened and a tall, dark man came out on the bridge wing. The man, perhaps the first mate, looked down directly at Lee, who continued to wave him away. Then, like a Latin Jesus, the guy put out his hand toward Lee. "Stay calm, man," he seemed to say. "Just chill out. Everything's going to be OK. We will save your miserable soul."

Though Lee still tried to wave off his rescuers, they paid no attention. "Oh God, get away from me," he screamed. "Sure as shit you're going to chop me up in your props. Just leave me alone!" But they couldn't hear him over the roar of the engines and the wind. And if they did understand what he was screaming, they ignored it.

By this time Lee had worked his way back to his raft, now floating amidships. But the position of the supply boat had changed relative to the seas. Captain Harold Roche had maneuvered his vessel downwind so that the raft was away from props and bow thruster. In this position the raft would be pushed toward the safest place to board. However, the seas were now coming from abeam, and the *Ducker* was rolling as if she were going to go over—right on top of Lee. He couldn't get away, and they wouldn't leave him in peace. So he would have to try to get onboard.

A row of tractor tires serving as fenders hung from chains fastened to welded rings just below the second deck. As the *Ducker* rolled away, the tires were jerked high in the air. When she rolled back toward the men in the raft, the tires plunged into the water in front of them. Hanging onto the lifeline running around the outside of the raft, Lee watched the movement of the tire nearest him, and the next time it plummeted, he grabbed the chain above it. Immediately he went soaring 30 feet in the air standing on top of the tire, then crashed back into the water, but with a steel grip on the chain. Once again he soared skyward, then crashed back down into the sea. He felt like he was being shot out of a gun, first in one direction, then the other. Still, he hung on, and the next time the *Ducker* lofted him into the air, he managed to grab a stanchion at eye level and hoist himself over the railing onto the second deck, where he flopped, exhausted.

After a couple of minutes just holding onto the railing and shaking, Lee climbed down the 8-foot ladder to the afterdeck. Hayman Webster, the mate, and another crewman were at a break on the starboard side where the railing had been removed for easy entry. They were trying to snatch men out of the raft in the split second when the *Ducker*'s deck was at water level. Lee took one of the life rings fastened with black polypropylene line to the railing and tossed it to someone in the raft. By taking in slack on the line when the *Ducker* rolled toward them, the men were then able to keep themselves opposite the break in the rail.

Shane was one of the first men to be hauled on deck. Then he and Lee and Webster began pulling in the others. One of them would act as the puller while the other two held on to the puller's waist to keep from being washed overboard. Clay Horschel and Danny Weidenboener were soon helping them pull other men onboard. At each plunge to sea level another man was grabbed, and as the *Ducker* swept into the air, they heaved him on deck. When every last soul had been plucked from the water, the men retreated to the galley or to the bridge, and Harold Roche gunned the *Ducker*, swung her around, and headed downwind to look for more survivors.

Within twenty minutes another raft was spotted a half-mile to the east with people waving from it. The *Ducker* went down into a trough, and when she rode up on the next crest, the raft had disappeared. The half-dozen men on the bridge, crew and survivors acting as lookouts, could find no sign of it. Then someone thought they saw it again, but the object turned out to be wreckage. After another five minutes, someone from on deck raced in and yelled that there was a raft behind them. They had overshot it.

Within a couple of minutes Harold had brought the pitching *Ducker* close to the raft. Keeping downwind of it and operating the vessel from a second set of aft-facing controls at the rear of the bridge, where he had a good view of the afterdeck, he was able to maintain position using both his bow thruster and the props at the stern. This maneuver required extraordinary skill, and some luck. He lined up the raft with the forward section of the afterdeck and tried to keep the ship just far enough away that the raft would not be crushed under the supply boat each time she rolled.

Hayman, along with Clay, Shane, Lee, and Lucio, one of the deckhands, was back on deck pulling in people from the raft. They had hauled in all but two or three men when Lucio, who had just guided a hollow-eyed survivor to the galley entrance and safety, was returning to the rail. The *Ducker* took an especially heavy roll to port and a wave of water roared over the already slippery deck. It washed Lucio off his feet, and before anyone could reach him, he was swept over the side and in seconds was in the *Ducker*'s wake.

The men on deck, who themselves had held on for their own lives and who had seen the young crewman washed overboard, yelled and pointed. Harold

had seen him go, too, but before he had time to do
anything besides take his engines out of gear, the next
wave picked up Lucio and carried him right back
onboard. The young sailor landed with a thud and
immediately was swept against the starboard bulwarks. Amazingly, aside from being bruised all over
his body, he was unhurt. The *Ducker* crew went back
to getting the rest of the men out of the raft. Some of
the men had been praying, because when the vessel
had stopped pulling them in, they thought they were
going to be abandoned by their rescuers. Captain
Harold Roche never considered it.

A few miles to the north of the *Ducker*, the *Carolina*
intermittently pitched over wave crests as she
searched for survivors. West perhaps a mile and a half,
the *Captain John* hunted in another area. The three
captains had had no opportunity to lay out a search
grid so they could systematically coordinate their
rescue efforts, but it turned out all right anyway. The
boats patrolled a rough line. The captains usually
knew where the other two vessels were in relation
to their own, and consciously they swept areas away
from the other boats.

The *Captain John* continued finding rafts, but
more often small groups of swimmers, their little life-
vest lights blinking like fireflies in a dark, turbulent

universe split only by wave crests and spume. In each case the massive steel tug was brought alongside the helpless men in the water with a precision that seemed impossible. Robert Trosclair handled the *Captain John* like a brain surgeon, so delicately did he control the movements of his vessel in the overpowering seas. Just a little too much power or too little, just a bit greater flick of the rudder toggle or not quite enough, and he would have killed the people he was trying to rescue. Nor was Trosclair the only magician. Richard Cassel on the *North Carolina* and Harold Roche on the *Ducker Tide* both controlled their larger and more unwieldy supply boats with similar precision.

The three captains were alike in other respects. All were Cajuns from western Louisiana. The name *Cajun* refers to people of Acadian French descent whose Catholic ancestors were driven out of the Acadian region of Nova Scotia by the British and who settled in southwestern Louisiana beginning in the 1760s. Hard-working small farmers, trappers, and fishermen, they often lived in the bayous, where the only practical transportation was by boat. So in many families youngsters were raised on the water and were taught how to handle small boats at an early age. The boys often became fishermen or got jobs on workboats supplying the new offshore oil industry. The three captains all were experienced watermen before they were old enough to shave.

Robert Trosclair, raised in the bayous southwest of Morgan City, fished for his family's dinner, hunted alligators, and was more at home on the water than on land. When he was sixteen he got his first job as a deckhand on a little tug of which Sam Smith was captain. They towed barges around the inland waterways. That was in 1950. They have worked together ever since.

Trosclair is lean and weathered and has a ready laugh. He makes friends easily and is a natural leader. Chuck Denning says he is the most dependable captain in the towboat industry. Robert calls himself an astronaut of the water. "I've worked all around," he says. "I've worked in the North Sea, shit, Rotterdam, England, Scotland, Singapore—towed pipe on a little boat over there along the coast of Malaysia and Thailand. I was down there two years, and when the job finished I came across the Pacific towing another tug with a small boat that was only about 75 feet long."

The other two captains are of the same mold. Richard Cassel, 5 feet 11 inches and of medium build, is confident and outgoing. People in the industry say he is a great captain. His weathered countenance reflects his many years at sea, mostly spent on oil supply vessels with the Seabulk Company.

Whereas Cassel grew up near Trosclair, Captain Harold Roche was raised farther west, in the small town of Kaplan. Born in 1947 to a family who suffered through hard times, Harold, along with his four brothers and sisters, worked from an early age to help put food on the table. As soon as Harold graduated from high school, he went into the Marine Corps. In 1968 he began as a deckhand for Tidewater Marine, working his way up to captain. Now the 6-foot-1-inch, 200-pound captain is distinguished and grey-bearded. Harold still sails for Tidewater, though for thirteen years he was their operations manager in Brazil. He is outgoing, with many close friends. They and his family respect his integrity. His daughter Tanya describes him as "just a good human being."

Harold and the other two captains are members of the small fraternity of Cajun captains known the world over for their fine ship handling—and if they hadn't proven it beyond doubt before, they were proving it now. But no matter how skilled they were, they could not perform rescues by themselves. They needed mates and crews to haul the survivors aboard while braving mountainous seas on unsheltered decks. With the *Captain John* and the *Ducker Tide*, this was not a problem. On the *North Carolina* it was.

The forty-five-year-old first mate of the *Carolina*, Eulalio Zapata Martinez, would not be considered an imposing figure. Of medium height, a little paunchy, and with round, babyish features, he might be a Mexican dry goods salesman. In fact he is a qualified tug captain who in the past has captained both tugs and supply boats. Eulalio has a calm, placid manner and a soft, respectful way of dealing with people. These qualities conceal a fierce dedication to his family and to his work. They also conceal a dogged determination to see a job through, a determination that would be severely tested in the hours ahead.

As the crew of the 269 jumped off the sinking barge, Richard Cassel had brought the *Carolina* downwind, where he expected the swimmers and the rafts to drift. The *Captain John* and the *Ducker Tide*, seen and then lost through the waves, were working to the south. Richard's crew cowered against the deckhouse as massive white cataracts coursed across the deck. Sometimes a wave captured a helpless deckhand, hurling him against the bulwarks or some piece of gear. A crewman would run out from behind the winch drum, or wherever he had found a handhold or a bit of shelter, to rescue a shipmate who had been slammed against the lee rail before he could be swept away. The *Carolina* was also rolling so far to one side, then the other, that they thought she might go over. Several times a deckhand just managed to prevent himself from being washed over the side.

During a brief lull, Eulalio Zapata told the crew to get ready to begin bringing survivors onboard. The other crew members on deck looked at each other, terrified. They already had come close to drowning when the *Carolina* had nearly capsized after the tow-line snagged in the towing bitts. Most of them had families at home. Eulalio says they yelled to him that they weren't going to take any more chances. "We have to," he yelled back. "Who else is going to save all those men?"

One after another, he says, the crew shook their heads. "You are paid more than we are. You save them."

A captain or mate cannot *order* men to jeopardize their lives in such dangerous conditions. The crew of the *Carolina* were right. For the three hundred dollars a month they made, why should they do anything but try to stay alive themselves? If they died at sea, who would take care of their families? No one. Eulalio despaired. He thought of his own wife and children in Tampico. Why should *he* risk his life any further? Then he saw two men in life preservers being swept past the *Carolina*, waving at him before they were covered by a wave.

In between breakers, Eulalio scrambled over to a storage locker near the entrance to the engine room and pulled out a small cargo net. He also grabbed two coils of half-inch nylon line. With his heart pounding and water streaming off him, he looped one line around him underneath his arms and tied it, then fastened the other end to an eye in front of the winch in the middle of the deck. That allowed him to get to either side. He cut the second nylon line into pieces and tied them along one side of the cargo net. Between waves he tried to fasten the net to hooks running under the starboard bulwarks so that it fell into the water next to the hull, but his hands were so numb he had trouble tying the knots.

Swimmers seemed to flash by in the sea; they were often gone before Cassel could maneuver the *Carolina* close enough for Zapata to throw them a line. To Eulalio, the men looked like floating bits of dunnage hurtling by him. Sometimes, leaning over the bulwarks, he reached out and grabbed someone, only to have a wave tear the screaming man out of his hands and carry him away. The man might emerge briefly before he was lost again. And sometimes the *Carolina* was surrounded by men in the water, to the point that it was impossible to maneuver the nearly 200-foot vessel without running over someone. And in each of the three captains' minds lurked the terrible

possibility that they would kill someone they were trying to rescue.

Victor Diaz, the lead dive tender, who had gone
off the port bow, described what happened to him
after he dove into the sea. "As I came back up I
opened my eyes; it was dark green. And when I actually came up I felt somebody fall directly behind me.
At that moment I swam away because I knew if they
would fall right on top of me, I would break my neck
and I wouldn't make it. At this moment a lot of the
men are just jumping into the sea, like if you would
be by a pond and you see the frogs leaping into the
pond. They were just flopping in. The tugboat and the
supply boat at this time, they were circling the barge
like two sharks over a prey, and what they wanted to
do was to pick up the men once they abandoned ship.
They would maneuver themselves to pick up the survivors. Getting into the water there were a lot of men.
And the waves and everything the way it was working,
you really had a hard time maneuvering yourself with
so many bodies in the water."

Victor continued with difficulty: "I was in the
water and the boat [*North Carolina*] was maneuvering
to pick up some of the men. There was a curtain of
men [around the boats]. And the stern [right in front
of me] had two giant propellers. A body had gone
through the propellers. The poor soul got sucked in.

And what landed an arm's length away was the head of the individual. The ocean was saturated with blood. I saw part of the face. It just came hanging from part of the neck itself, so I didn't get a full view of the face. After that happened I just swam away. There was no way I was going to be ground up."

Victor went on to explain that the men on the *Carolina* never even saw the man at the stern. There were so many swimmers around it at that particular time that it was impossible for the captain or the boat's crew to keep track of them all.

Victor just started swimming off by himself. "I figured I'll just take my chances at sea. And [after a while] I just happened to see another man and then another one. So we became a human chain. We basically grabbed each other by the [life] vests. As we were floating, one of the many fears, once blood is in the ocean, the first thing that's attracted are sharks."

Although Victor and his group, which eventually numbered twelve men, never saw sharks, they had all they could do to battle the sea. Victor continued, "At times we were spread out and at times we were in a circle, and it all depended, because sometimes as we would ride a wave up and it would tumble over, we would fall with it and it plunged us underneath. [Then] we broke the chain as we surfaced. We gathered ourselves as much as we could trying to become the human chain again. It was an exhausting process. And as it was happening—we were plunged under— we had no idea which was up or down. When I was pushed beneath the surface I swallowed a great deal of saltwater. There was a time that I couldn't even taste it anymore. It just became regular fresh water in my mouth.

"We drifted a great deal of distance, 'cause I remember looking and the silhouette of the barge was there one minute and it was gone the next. We drifted for quite a distance, and on the horizon every time we would rise on top of a swell we could see the searchlights of the vessels as they were trying to pick up people. The vest that I had was torn on the right-hand side, and the water was saturating it [so] that it kept pulling me forward. So I would grab a man, put him in front of me to hold me upright." Victor and his human chain continued to drift through the night.

With Eulalio Zapata still by himself on the afterdeck, Richard Cassel tried to bring the *Carolina* on the lee side of a swimmer so that the man would be swept into them. Sometimes this was on the side where the cargo net hung, and then the swimmer might be able to climb the net by himself, or at least with Zapata's help. Just as frequently, however, a man drifted into the port side, and then the mate had to lean far over the bulwarks, grasping the man by the arm, the life preserver, the shirt, even by the hair, and haul him over the side. Rescued men on deck knelt, crying and thanking God. A couple of guys hugged each other, sobbing over their salvation. Some were like zombies, lethargic and in shock. They staggered aimlessly around the deck until one of the seamen leaped out, scrambling over the slippery, careening deck, and led them below before they could get washed back over the rail. Once in a while one or two of the *Carolina's* crew dashed out and tossed a preserver at the end of a line to a man in the sea, then darted back to the safety of the deckhouse. For the most part, though, Eulalio says he was alone at the rail, single-handedly bringing people onboard.

Zapata felt like a tightrope walker as he tried to pull people in; one false step and he'd be over the side. And just as he feared, his luck soon ran out. He was reaching out to a swimmer when a wave lifted him right over the bulwarks. Hanging from his safety line, he fought and clawed, trying to pull himself back onboard.

While he was dangling over the side, one of the deckhands who had seen him go over slipped out and threw him a life preserver, then scuttled back to safety. The life preserver trailed in the water, far out of Eulalio's grasp. Finally he was able to pull himself back over the rail, where he knelt and clutched a stanchion until he could regain his strength. The next time he was swept overboard he landed right on top of the cargo net and was able to climb back on deck fairly easily. Still, he did not know how much more he could take. He felt himself getting weaker and weaker. But in a strange way he had forgotten his fear. He had forgotten his family. He had forgotten everything but what he knew he had to do: grab the frightened swimmers and bring them onboard.

One man that Zapata rescued would always stand out in his mind. Santos Pitalua Mazaba was a rigger on the 269. He had one of the flat life jackets with little flotation left, so he had been forced to swim to keep himself afloat. By the time the *Carolina* found him, Santos was exhausted and had no strength left in his arms. Also, he was heavy and not in good physical condition. When Eulalio saw Santos in the water, he threw him a line and pulled him in close to the tug. Still holding the line, Zapata reached down to grasp Pitalua's arm. It was slippery, coated with oil, and he couldn't maintain a grip on it. The boat rolled away, and when it rolled back, Eulalio reached out again to grab his hand. The rigger stuck the line in his mouth so that he would have both hands free to grasp Eulalio's outstretched hand. As the tug began to roll away again, only the line held Santos to the vessel.

Before he could grab it again, he was jerked away from the *Carolina* and the line tore out all his front teeth. Another large wave swept Santos back toward the tug's deck, and that momentum finally enabled Eulalio to haul him in over the side.

Santos lay bleeding on the deck. As Eulalio got him to his feet and steered him below, he asked, "Are you going to be all right?" Though blood was still gushing out of his mouth, Santos replied, "*Si, gracias*. My teeth I can replace, but not my life."

As the *Carolina* worked her end of the ragged line formed by the three rescue boats, she seemed to be finding just swimmers, no life rafts. So Zapata dealt with the men one by one, until another big wave exploded into the *Carolina*. Eulalio went over the side again in a tidal wave of water. The lifeline cut into his ribs, almost tearing him in half, as the next wave slammed him back into the supply boat's hull. He swung in the air like a side of beef, then plunged beneath the surface as the *Carolina* rolled in another wave. Eulalio was on the side opposite the cargo net, and he couldn't turn himself around to grab the rail. Each time he tried, another wave sucked him under-water, and when he emerged all he could do was try to clear his lungs. He coughed and sputtered and thought he was dying as once more he plunged into the sea.

Eventually a wave spun Eulalio on his lifeline so that his hands could grasp the bulwarks and he managed to climb onboard, where he collapsed on deck. Cassel, at the rear steering station, had seen him go overboard again but was unable to leave the helm. Now he called out over the loudspeaker, "Zapata, you OK?" Eulalio looked up and nodded weakly, but had a hard time regaining his feet.

Fortunately, a young Mexican deckhand from the 269 whom he had rescued earlier had come back out to help. Zapata found another safety line for the crewman, and for a while the two men worked together. Then two of the rescued American dive crew also came out. Eventually a third crewman joined them, and these four men took over the rescue work, letting the weary Eulalio retire to the wheelhouse.

The overloaded raft with Phil Richard, Mitch Pheffer, Chuck Rountree, Ray Pepperday, and two dozen others had not been drifting long when it was suddenly illuminated by a searchlight. Before the groggy survivors knew it, the *Captain John* was just in front of them. Mitch watched as the tug's stern pitched out of the water and the boat's screws screamed in his face. Trosclair swung the stern away and soon the raft was alongside. One after another the men bounded onboard. The last four still in the raft as a wave started to push it away from the tug were Phil, Mitch, Chuck, and a guy in the bottom who seemed unconscious. At the last second Phil leaped onto the deck. But then the raft again drifted back toward the *John*'s stern and her thrashing propellers. Another wave momentarily swept the raft toward the tug, and Mitch, realizing that this might be his last chance to get aboard, jumped.

"I grabbed the rail [the bulwarks]," he remembered, "but I couldn't pull myself over the side. My legs are hanging in the water. I've got my wetsuit and my work boots on, and I don't have the strength to pull myself over. One moment I'm underwater; the next moment Phil grabs me and pulls me over, and he falls down. I turned right around because I knew that Chuck was still in the raft and it was drifting back toward the propellers. I just looked at Chuck. Chuck and I looked at each other and I said, 'Jump, man.' It was too far and he couldn't make it. But Chuck jumped and we locked hands. Chuck is hanging in the waves and our hands are locked. We rode the waves out. They covered our heads and Chuck is still hanging down. I couldn't pull him over. I didn't have enough strength. Then Phil is back and pulls Chuck over and the three of us go rolling around on the deck."

After the men boarded the *Captain John*, there was still a crewman left in the raft who had not gotten to his feet. He did not move but stared up with sightless eyes from inside a 4-foot pool of water in the raft's center. His mouth open, with a look of horror on his face, Angel, the young Mexican radio operator, had drowned in their midst, and no one had even noticed. Evidently he had slipped beneath the surface of the pool and been unable to call out or to claw his way past all the men on top of him.

Quickly they grabbed the raft and brought Angel into a cabin where they stretched him out on his back. After clearing his airways, the 269's doctor, Raymundo Hernandez Isidro, a forty-year-old physician from Veracruz who had already been taken onboard, began to give him artificial respiration. The doctor worked steadily, trying desperately to bring even a spark of life back into that motionless young body. After three-quarters of an hour of devoted effort, Dr. Isidro stopped, realizing he had failed. The doctor seemed to die as well. He went off into a corner and sat in a stupor, staring into space.

The *Captain John* continued to find and pick up survivors. When they sighted the next raft, Robert Trosclair left the wheelhouse and took the controls in the glassed-in doghouse. It sat on the aft end of the bridge deck facing out over the stern. With its complete set of controls Trosclair could operate his tug as well from there as he could from the bridge. Lorenzo Wilson kept the searchlight on the men in the water and maintained control on the bridge until Robert reached the doghouse. Then Lorenzo scrambled down to take charge on deck.

As the *Captain John* rode up a big wave, Robert feathered his props, reducing power, and took his engines out of gear. If the props of the tug or of either of the supply boats were out of the water when the boats were under full power, an automatic override, an integral part of the controls of most large vessels, would shut the engines down to keep them from overrevving and destroying a bearing or breaking a shaft. An inadvertent engine shutdown at the wrong time in hurricane seas could jeopardize the safety of the vessel. On the other hand, an override failure could cause them to lose both their engines at a critical time. Either situation was to be avoided, and the captains, as a matter of course, cut back their power each time the props came out of the water. With waves staggering the vessels every few seconds, maneuvering throttles was a constant and demanding part of maintaining control of the ships.

Trosclair resumed power once the tug's stern was back in the water and brought the *Captain John* to within about 10 feet upwind of the raft, keeping it in his lee. Then Robert reduced power and put his engines out of gear again, but just briefly. He had to hold position so he would not be pushed on top of the raft. However, he was also faced with possibly sucking the raft into the near Kort nozzle and the massive propeller inside it as the tug rolled, bringing the near-side propeller very close to the surface. So every time he approached a raft or a swimmer, he left the near-side engine out of gear.

The deckhands had knotted some 1-inch nylon lines and tossed them toward the raft, one minute near the tug's deck level and the next bobbing 25 feet beneath it. The first man grabbed a knotted line and was quickly hauled on deck. The next fellow got a grip on a line, but before the crew could haul him in over the bulwarks another wave swelled under the tug, pushing it high above the Mexican dangling on the end of his rope. Lorenzo screamed at him in Spanish not to let go, for if he did he would get sucked right under the tug. Together the crew yanked the petrified man onboard and then had to wrestle the line out of his hands.

Their timing seemed off, for the next two men also were left dangling, but somehow Lorenzo and the crew were able to bring them aboard. During all this, wave crests were breaking over the *John*'s wheelhouse roof and cascading over the afterdeck. Somebody would shout a warning and the sailors would grab a stanchion or any handhold they could find to keep from getting washed over the side. Finally all the men from the raft were onboard. Robert and Lorenzo returned to the wheelhouse and the crew collapsed around the survivors, who were beginning to fill every nook and cranny of the tug's interior.

Phil Richard and Mitch Pheffer, the two young divers, then took over rescue duties from the exhausted crew. Each time they saw a light or someone in the water, they ran up to the wheelhouse and pointed out the location to Robert, who would then move to the doghouse. Chuck stayed in the wheelhouse and acted as lookout. The rest of the night Phil and Mitch, by themselves, worked the afterdeck, pulling in one survivor after another. When a wave came, one or the other would yell a warning and they would grab whatever was handy. Phil remembered, "Tugboats have huge, huge cleats that you could wrap your arms and legs around. I would wrap myself around one of those, in the fetal position, and the deck of the tug would go underwater for what seemed like an eternity. I would sit there underwater and go 'One-Mississippi, two-Mississippi, three-Mississippi.' I would hold my breath and finally the son of a bitch would pop back out of the water. I was puking up sea-water for days after that."

For hours Phil and Mitch kept pulling people in. Some were covered with oil and were nearly impossible to grab. Others were so weary they were unable to help themselves in any way. One of the last people the tug came across was Victor Diaz.

Robert Trosclair, at the helm, saw something in the water reflecting the glare from the tug's searchlight. As he brought his vessel closer he could see that it was a group of men—it was Victor's human chain. Victor described it: "Finally after a great deal of just hoping and praying, the tugboat managed to see a reflection off the vests. We were told they spotted us because we were in a group. The searchlight hit the reflectors and they saw that it was a group of us. As it was getting closer and closer, the tugboat was swallowed up, literally, by a wave, just completely, and it's like you would see a submarine piercing through the surface. That's what the tug looked like, and it finally shut its engines off. There were two people, Americans, and they were screaming, 'One at a time, one at a time!' What they had done is taken a rope and they had put knots in it and they had launched it in our group, and we all managed to be pulled onboard by these guys, who risked themselves being sucked over."

Victor continued, "Once I was onboard they had to drag me inside the tugboat and I stood there. I wanted to scream. I wanted to laugh. I wanted to cry. But not a word came out of me. I stood there not even moving. They had a jug of fresh water, and as each individual was rescued and pulled in, they were given the fresh water. As I drank it, the first thing I did, I puked it basically all out, and it was a lot of the saltwater that I had ingested that was still in my gut."

Victor was led below. He found a place on the deck in the engine room, squeezed between vomiting, oil-covered survivors. There he collapsed.

Chapter Eight

❧

L ENN COBB and the others in his raft didn't know how much longer they could survive. Waves continued to hammer them with such ferocity that some men were not able to completely expel water from their airways between dunkings. A couple of crewmen coughed and vomited so much they seemed on the verge of drowning. Lenn himself, after the dolphins had gone, lost track of time. He continued to look toward the waves in order to judge when they would next be stuffed under the surface and when he could get an extra breath. As they rode up one wave crest Lenn looked out to see a body bobbing next to the raft. It was strangely familiar. With a start he realized he was looking at Jim Vines, lifeless, floating alongside them. Lenn remembered seeing him when they were about ready to jump off the barge. At the last second Jim had retreated back over the rail instead of jumping off with the divers, who had promised to watch over him. For years the two images, one of Jim on deck and the other of him bobbing in the water, would run through Lenn like an electric shock. Vines's body soon floated out of sight.

Lenn and the others could sometimes see one or the other of the rescue boats as they pitched and tossed, looking as much like potential victims as rescuers. Along with many of his fellow survivors, Lenn didn't think they could safely get onboard under those conditions. "When the *North Carolina* spotted us," he remembered, "they brought the boat alongside. And in those seas it was wild. One minute you're looking at the antennas on the top of the boat and the next minute you're seeing the propellers turning. It didn't look good. I was thinking that our chances would be better if we just hung on in our life raft.

"It seemed like we could get swept under the supply boat real easy—but the way the guy [Richard Cassel] did it, he got the boat between us and the seas and then let the seas wash him into us with his engines out of gear. He just drifted into us. He did a hell of a job."

When their raft got close enough to the *Carolina*, men started jumping from it onto the big airplane tires that were used as fenders and ringed the vessel just above water level. With each wave, Eulalio and a young Mexican crewman of the 269 who was never identified, dodging waves and with little regard for their own safety, grabbed the survivors, sometimes tackling them to keep them from being carried back into the ocean.

Lenn was the last off the raft. After jumping on a tire he was tossed into the air and landed on his back, sliding along the deck like a shuffleboard puck until one of the crew grabbed him. As the *Carolina* came down into the next trough, the empty life raft was sucked under it. In a second the raft exploded and was spat out by the vessel's props in a hundred pieces. As Lenn said, their rescue was a one-shot deal.

The *North Carolina* forged on, searchlights piercing the night, probing the wave-tossed seas for any signs of life. As the search continued, so did the ship continue to be pounded. Life-raft canisters, railings, antennas, and other gear were torn apart and washed overboard. The hammering of the waves never stopped, but it was at its worst when Cassel swung the *Carolina* broadside to the seas, sacrificing the vessel to pick up survivors. The *Carolina* would go over so far that the lee rails were nearly underwater, and some of the newly rescued wondered if they might be on two sinking vessels in one night.

The *Carolina* persevered, however, heaving to whenever there were men to be picked up. Eventually there were no more rafts to be seen, just swimmers in small groups, three or four or five or, a couple of times, seven or eight men, lashed to each other. Occasionally a lone, frightened man afloat in his orange life vest would impossibly appear in the enormous breaking seas. It seemed a miracle when a lonely little bobber, just a human pinprick in the maelstrom, was spotted.

The divers, still with the protection of their wetsuits, had taken over rescue duties from the young crewman and the exhausted Eulalio Zapata. Roy Cline, one of the two dive supervisors, Rob Whaley, Kris Nielsen, and Rob Boettger, along with Lenn, positioned themselves on the aft end of the bridge deck. If any of them happened to see a man in the water who was not visible to Captain Richard Cassel or to those who were spotting for him in the wheelhouse, they would run in and point out the swimmer's location.

Richard had the same aft control station on the *Carolina* that Harold Roche did on the *Ducker Tide*. When the *Carolina* approached a swimmer, Richard took the conn at the aft end of the pilothouse, and the divers went down the ladder to the place on the afterdeck where the bulwarks broke to provide a deck-level entry.

As the swimmers came alongside the *Carolina*, the divers would toss out life rings to them. Then, with other guys holding on to them, they would pull a swimmer on deck. Sometimes two divers would be grabbing two swimmers at once. At other times the men in the water were able to latch onto a tire, but as the hours passed, those still waterborne had been battling the elements for so long, swallowing seawater and occasionally being coated with oil, that they were unable to function. Then all the effort would have to come from those on deck.

One of the men who floated by was Rozy, Ron Rozmarynoski, the life-support tech from Sturgeon Bay, Wisconsin. He had broken his leg when he jumped off the 269 with Kevin Dumont. The two men had lost track of each other immediately upon hitting the water, and Rozy had been by himself a long time. He was in a bad way and had gone into shock. After fishing him out of the water, Lenn untied a little ditty bag lashed to his wrist and tossed it into a corner. Lenn and one of the other divers were helping the nearly incoherent Rozy, one supporting each shoulder, taking him to shelter. But Rozy kept hollering, "Find my ditty bag." Thinking that he might have his valuables in it, Lenn asked him, "Do you have money in it?" "No, it's got my cigarettes!" Feeling sorry for Rozy, who on top of everything else was going through nicotine withdrawal, someone brought him some fresh cigarettes before helping him go below. Rozy asked if they had found Kevin, but nobody had seen him.

When Kevin hit the water, he looked around for Rozy and, not finding him, began swimming as hard as he could to put distance between himself and the sinking barge. He had not gotten far when his legs tangled in something under the surface. Thrashing, he tried to kick free but couldn't. Then he realized he was tangled in a line and it was attached to something, maybe the barge, in which case he was in big trouble. He continued thrashing, trying to free himself, but all he did was cause the tangles to tighten around his legs. Each time a wave swept by he was sucked beneath the surface. He sputtered, choking with water in his lungs, bobbed up long enough to cough it out and to take a quick breath before he was again plunged back under—mouth closed but water still getting in his lungs—and pushed to the surface once more. The routine continued and each time the terrified man, now incapable of most movement, choked more and inhaled less air. It seemed very likely that he would drown. Finally he happened to break the surface facing downwind long enough to expel most of the water in his lungs.

Kevin glanced over his shoulder, looking for the next wave. Only the tip of the 269's bow and her crane were still visible above the sea. Out of the corner of his eye he saw a monster wave sweeping toward him. Just as it engulfed him, the water exploded, and like magic, a life raft mushroomed up next to him, roughly shoving him out of its way. The raft canisters were fitted with hydrostatic release units and evidently the large wave stuffed the canister far enough below the surface to release its raft. Kevin grabbed a lifeline fastened around the raft. His legs had been tangled in the raft's tether to the canister still attached to the sunken 269. As the barge settled deeper in the water, the tension on the line had increased until finally it set off the automatic release, which produced the explosive inflation and snapped the tether.

Now Kevin was floating free with his own life raft, but, in shock, he was too weak to climb the ladder to the raft's opening. So he hung on and bobbed as waves swept him and his savior downwind. Once he caught his breath, he again tried and failed to climb the ladder. Then he started working his way around the raft's perimeter. He had thought he was alone, but as he came around the raft he found a Mexican galley hand who, unseen, had been swimming nearby. When the raft popped up near him, he grabbed it and had been clinging to the far side. Kevin was still trying desperately to climb the high-sided walls of the empty raft. The galley hand yelled to him, "Take it easy. Take it easy. *Oye, mira. El barco esta aqui!*" And sure enough, as he turned, he could see the *Captain John* pitching over the waves coming toward them.

At the helm, Trosclair saw the raft, but it appeared to be empty. He was starting to turn the tug away when Lorenzo Wilson suggested, "Don't you think we should check?" Trosclair agreed and brought the stern back around toward what he was sure was an empty raft while the mate headed down the ladder to the afterdeck. Phil Richard and Mitch Pheffer were already there peering at the raft. "Captain Robert," Phil shouted up, "there's guys here!"

Kevin watched apprehensively as the *Captain John* drifted down upon him, stern first, with the three huge props boiling out of the water on each wave crest. Sometimes the tug rose until the stern was at a 45-degree angle above the bow. The roar of the props deafened him. "I'm ground meat," he thought. But at the last second Trosclair powered the stern away and Kevin was alongside a break in the afterdeck on the starboard side.

The Mexican galley hand eagerly brought himself

aboard with a line that was thrown him, but Kevin was so weak he couldn't even grasp the line. Then Mitch and Phil were grabbing him by the back of the pants. With a mighty heave they flung Kevin on deck. Still Kevin couldn't move. He lay there helplessly. Over the loudspeaker Captain Robert shouted, "Get that man off the deck. Get him inside!" Two deck-hands half carried him through the door to the engine room. There he was set down on a grate above the diesels, where he lost consciousness.

The men of the 269 may have thought that they had been entirely overlooked by the outside world, but they had not. The District 8 Coast Guard headquarters in New Orleans coordinates rescue work for the Gulf of Mexico. At 1615 Sunday they received North Bank's distress call and subsequent reports from the *Captain John* and from C.C.C.'s headquarters in Carmen. The District 8 control center directed its air station at the Clearwater–St. Petersburg (Florida) airport to launch a C-130 Hercules search-and-rescue aircraft, but for unaccountable reasons, their order did not go out until seven hours after the distress call was radioed. Perhaps it was that a Mayday had never been declared. In any case, even with a prompt take-off, the search-and-rescue plane could not have reached the scene before dark.

Lt. Commander James Cullinan, now an Alaska Airlines pilot, was duty aircraft commander that night. After notifying his crew of the projected launch, he went to the unit's weather computer, which had a direct satellite feed. Jim Cullinan zeroed in on the Yucatan channel and plotted the last known position of the 269: less than 100 miles from the eye of Hurricane Roxanne. Under such poor weather conditions, a nighttime rescue by the C-130 seemed impossible. The plane's raft-drop altitude was 200 feet, and with 75-mile-an-hour winds, 40-foot seas, and almost no visibility, it would be unlikely that they could find anyone not already in a raft, and if by chance they did, just as unlikely that they could get a raft to the swimmer. Cullinan thought they would probably end up wasting rafts.

The commander spoke to some other search-and-rescue pilots, who concurred with his analysis and agreed that he should wait to launch so that the C-130 would be over the area at first light on Monday the sixteenth. With three hours of transit time, that would mean an 0200 liftoff. Since it was already nearing 2300, that seemed like the best plan, but when Cullinan called New Orleans control, the operations officer there told him to go stick his nose in it. Reluctantly Cullinan prepared to launch. Then he received a countermanding order from New Orleans to take off for an 0500 arrival at the scene. He and his crew would get a couple of hours of sleep before takeoff.

Gustavo Zaldivar, the storekeeper, floated in the waves with a group of swimmers. Someone had a 30-inch-diameter life ring, and three men were clinging to it. Another person had a piece of hawser, which had been looped through the life ring so that they could stay together. Others joined them.

Earlier that day on the 269 when Gustavo and El Padre had been released from the bucket brigade, Gustavo had gone up on deck. He had stayed on the heliodeck for a while, then worked his way back to about midships on the port side. It is not known where El Padre stayed during the afternoon or when or where he jumped into the sea.

But when men around Gustavo began jumping in, he did too. He remembered hitting the water and, after bobbing back to the surface, striking out to get away from the barge. Within a few minutes he was carried by the current, but he became fearful of barrels and planks sweeping down on top of him. He began facing the oncoming waves so that at least he would have a little warning of something that might smash into him. Perhaps he could duck under it or at least shove it away.

More men kept joining his group, and eventually

there were eleven of them holding onto either the hawser or the life ring itself. Waves would hit the group and tear off one or two of the swimmers, who would then have to paddle furiously to get back to the others.

When they had been in the water perhaps two hours, a big wave hit them. Gustavo was carried away from the others. He came out of a trough choking and spewing saltwater. However, the swimmers around the life ring had vanished. He looked all over but couldn't see them, so he just floated on by himself. It was frightening being alone, but there wasn't anything he could do about it. Night had reduced visibility from poor to nothing. He felt he would not be seen alone, a little cork afloat in the sea. All he could do was to try to keep from swallowing saltwater. He began to pray to God to take care of his family when he died.

Gustavo was by himself for more than an hour, and then right in front of him appeared his old group of swimmers with their life ring. Joyously he rejoined them. A couple of the guys gave him quick smiles of greeting between waves. Shortly after he was back with the group, a searchlight lit up the water around them. They all waved like crazy, and soon the *Ducker Tide* came up to windward. Amazingly, all eleven were still together after three hours in the water.

The *Ducker* was rolling heavily, and each time her lee rail went into the sea, one or two of the men would grab lines holding tractor tires along the vessel's side and go shooting into the air standing on the inside of the tires as the tug rolled back onto a crest. Soon it was Gustavo's turn. He latched onto a line just above a tire and zoomed skyward. Before he could go smashing back into the following trough, two deckhands took hold of his arms and hauled him over the bulwarks. He staggered across the deck and through the aft door leading to the cabins. Just inside the passageway he joined a multitude of heaving, wretching survivors, who sprawled along both bulkheads. Gustavo never saw his fellow storekeeper, El Padre, again.

No one knows what happened to El Padre between the time he went topside on the barge and the time he was spotted, late in the evening, by men on the *Ducker Tide*. One of the 269's crew who had already been rescued and was helping to pull other survivors on deck saw the Father floating with an unconscious man in his arms. How long they had been in the sea and the circumstances that brought El Padre to take charge of the man—or even who the person was—remain a mystery.

A *Ducker* deckhand was using a boat hook to bring swimmers close to the vessel. Hooking the straps that cinched their life jackets, he would pull them close enough so that others could grab them. Both El Padre and the man in his arms were wearing the old flat work vests, with little buoyancy. They were on the lee side of the supply boat. The crewman with the boat hook pulled the two close to the hull, where the Father could have left the man he was supporting and taken hold of the eager hands reaching out to him. Instead he pushed his unconscious companion into the arms of the rescuers. The comatose crewman was hoisted aboard the *Ducker* and rushed below. Evidently he regained consciousness but afterward was lost in the throng of survivors and never knew what happened to the person who had saved his life.

The next time the vessel's lee rail rolled into the water, the deckhand with the boat hook managed to snag it in the back of El Padre's life jacket. As the ship rolled back toward vertical on the following wave, El Padre was pulled against the hull. Then just as men leaned over the side to grab him, his life jacket split where the boat hook had held it. Before anyone could do anything, the Father had slid down the side of the hull back toward the propellers, which because of the boat's roll were nearing the surface. There was no scream. There was no sound at all other than the noise of the thrashing props and the wind and waves.

In the next few moments all that surfaced were dozens of pieces of the life vest El Padre had been wearing. The vest could only have been shredded by being sucked into one of the propellers, and most certainly that is what happened to the Father. Those on deck looked at each other in shock. They searched for the body, but no signs of it were ever seen. Eventually the *Ducker* moved off, looking for others in the darkness.

One group of unlucky swimmers had drifted far to the east, almost 18 miles from where the 269 had gone down. Tim Noble, O. P. Chauvin, and the seven Mexican crewmen who were tied together wondered if they were ever going to be rescued. They felt very much alone, and they were. The three rescue vessels, if they could be seen at all, were just distant lights visible only briefly from wave crests. The string of men floated along, getting colder and weaker. They had been slammed by waves for nearly four hours, and that had taken its toll, draining them of energy. Then, when some of them had nearly given up, it finally was their turn. A spotlight lit them up like Times Square at midnight and the *North Carolina* came charging down on them. She looked like she was going to run them over. But at the last second, Richard Cassel reversed his stern props, and when the string of men next resurfaced after their plunge beneath the *North Carolina*'s bow wave, they found themselves along her starboard side, two-thirds of the way aft, next to the opening in her bulwarks. All nine men scrambled mightily to get on the supply boat. Two of the swimmers grabbed Noble, trying to use him as a lever to get closer to the *Carolina*. He dodged out of their grasp. He could see Rob Whaley, Lenn Cobb, Rob Boettger, and some others on deck throwing life rings to them and pulling guys onboard.

It took three tries for Tim to grab one of the big tires along the vessel's side and pull himself up on it. Then with his feet on the inside of the tire and hanging on to the chain from which the tire hung, he paused to rest. Lenn and Rob Whaley came over and tried to grab him, but Tim refused to let go of his tire. They were adamant that he allow them to pull him in. Just as adamantly he refused. Finally he took a breath and climbed over the rail. They half pulled him and he half stumbled to the deck, where he immediately began to vomit saltwater.

When Tim had a chance to collect himself, he began to look around for the rest of the men who had been with him. Besides the eight or nine crewmen and divers on the afterdeck, Tim spotted the others in his group—with one notable exception. O. P. Chauvin was missing. Noble went tearing around trying to find

Opie. He was not onboard. No one had seen him. Somehow he had gotten left. Tim went charging up to the wheelhouse to alert the captain and to put everyone on the lookout for him.

Ordwayne Paul Chauvin, part Cajun and part Homa Indian, whose family were neighbors of Lee Lloyd's in Louisiana, was called O. P. or Opie. He was a popular member of the dive crew. Opie and Ray Pepperday were the mechanics who kept the specialized diving equipment operational—as well as the heating, refrigeration, gas generation, and electrical systems of the saturation chamber and the diving bell. Lee said Opie could repair anything and besides that he was a wonderful artist. At forty-nine and with a bit of a belly, however, the balding man was not one of the athletes of the dive crew. Yet what he underwent between the time he left the 269 and the time he was rescued would have taxed the endurance and stamina of even the most physically fit.

Opie had gone off the barge from the starboard or low side, forward of the control tower. He had jumped with John Wheeler, the young life-support tech, but shortly after they hit the water they became separated. Opie watched men in a couple of nearby rafts being bombarded by human bodies leaping from the 269 and landing on top of them in their blind desire for a place in a raft. He thought he would be safer in the water, so he made no attempt to reach a raft. He was to regret this decision almost immediately, because he had one of the old work vests. Opie remembered it distinctly. "When I dove in, a lot of debris was in the water already, planks and oil and everything else. I saw one of the [dive] crew members passing me and he said, 'Hey, man, come on. Let's go.' So I tried to swim—which I can hardly do anyway. I kind of drifted along and grabbed a large piece of wood. It was a bunch of 4-by-4s made into a plank. So I held onto that, but the current was pushing me into the barge."

He shoved off with his hands and only succeeded in cutting himself on barnacles beneath the waterline. Then he turned around and tried pushing off with his feet. "I was all beat up when I finally got away," he said. "I looked back as I was drifting away and I could see the derrick still facing me. As I was drifting, the waves would come and hit me in the back, and each time I would go under. I felt like the toy bird that you put next to a glass [of water], you know, and that keeps ducking into the glass. I could see the barge slowly disappearing away from me."

After a while Opie saw three Mexican crewmen clinging to an orange Norwegian buoy. He joined them, and together they floated along holding on to his wood and the big round buoy. One of the Mexicans had a life jacket with no flotation remaining, so he took over Opie's plank, which was full of nails. One of the other two Mexicans seemed to be only half breathing and nearly unconscious. The four men also had a big piece of hawser between them, but it was covered with oil and grease. Shortly after Opie came across the three crewmen, Tim Noble and four others drifted up and Tim tied them all together.

The men continued to drift. Tim tried to attract the attention of one of the rescue vessels using his flashlight to signal them, but with no success. Two of the men became hysterical, sobbing, screaming, and grabbing at the swimmers nearest them. Tim, Opie, and the others tried to calm them and to stay out of their reach.

Finally the *North Carolina* saw them and came over. The bow wave pushed them under and then down the vessel's starboard side. Three of the guys Opie was tied to thrashed wildly to get to the *Carolina*. Fearful that they would pull him under, Opie untied himself from the line binding them together. He watched the others scramble over the side, but by the time it was his turn he had drifted off from the vessel. He was caught in a strong current that propelled him quickly away from any chance to get onboard. Opie tried to kick and stroke toward the supply boat but just kept getting carried farther and farther away. The men on the ship didn't see him, and soon the props boiled at the stern. The boat seemed to be searching for him, crisscrossing an area downwind. He tried as best he could to get their attention, waving and halfheartedly calling out over a wind that was so loud he knew he couldn't be heard. Eventually the *Carolina* sailed away, and he was all alone.

Drifting by himself, Opie thought that the *Carolina* would never be able to find him, a little speck in the middle of the night in overpowering seas. He says he had the feeling that no boat would find him. "I made my peace with God. I told Him, 'God, if you need to take me, go ahead.' I mean, there was nothing else."

Opie did have one small piece of luck, though. While they were still on the 269, he mentioned to Rozy that he had no light on his vest. Rozy said, "Hey, I found this light in my room. Take it." He took the light and fastened it to his life vest. So at least he had that. Opie drifted for what he guessed was about an hour and suddenly there was another searchlight beating the water around him. It was the *Ducker Tide*. As soon as their light hit him, he could see guys on deck jumping up and down and pointing at him. So maybe they *had* been looking for him.

The *Ducker* stopped right in front of him, so close he reached out and put his hand on its bow. It was like putting a hand on the corner of a thirty-story office tower that threatened to collapse on top of him. Opie tried to hold on to the stem, the bow's leading edge, but he was swept around it along the boat's opposite side. Someone threw him a line. It plopped into the water next to him, but it went slipping right through his hands. The next line thrown toward him fell far short. Within seconds Opie had drifted the length of the *Ducker* and was back by the props, close to the stern. He became frightened. The propellers were vibrating furiously. As the boat went over a wave, they would come partially out of the water. Opie thought his teeth would fall out, the vibration shook him so much. And he was terrified of getting drawn into those huge boiling props.

He started dog paddling, then tried swimming on his back, straining any way he could to get away from those menacing propellers. The *Ducker* turned away from him. The men onboard were searching everywhere for him, but they didn't see him. They feared he had been pulled under the hull and ground up into fish chum. The boat slowly headed off, searchlights shining everywhere but on him.

Opie despaired. He would never be rescued, and now he was quickly getting tired. His legs and arms could barely move. He was a smoker, heavier than he would have liked, and, as he had told others, not in 100 percent good shape. So even if he was spotted again, he didn't think he would have the strength to climb on a boat. In any case, he had no options, so he just drifted along. But by now both the supply boats were looking for him, the two captains in radio contact. Richard Cassel on the *North Carolina* reported that they had tried to pick up Opie but had lost him. Then Harold Roche on the *Ducker* came on and said the same thing had happened with his boat. The two ships were crisscrossing the area, searching for him.

It was the *Carolina* that spotted him again. It sailed up with spotlight blazing. Opie could see men on the foredeck pointing and yelling, "There he is! There he is!" Soon he was next to the break in the bulwarks along the afterdeck and someone was throwing him another line. Only this line, thank God, *this* line had knots in it every foot or so.

Opie grabbed the line with every ounce of strength he had left. No way was he going to let go of it this time. With the line in both hands he got pulled in until he hit the side of the hull. His back was up against it, and he was being slammed into it over and over as the *Carolina* repeatedly was hit broadside by waves. But he wouldn't let go of the rope. Water swept over the deck and gushed down on him. Still he wouldn't let loose of it. The boat continued to roll, and Opie, under the hull as the *Carolina* rolled on its beam ends, was still getting smashed into the hull and away, into it and away. Water continued pouring on top of him.

With the *Carolina* rolling so badly, first one rail in the water and then the other, the men who were trying to pull Opie in had to stop and grab whatever they could to keep themselves from being thrown into the sea. Finally three of them were able to yank him in.

But Opie was wounded, cut from head to toe. Barnacles, first on the 269, then on the *Ducker*, had made mincemeat of his skin. Once onboard, he sprawled on deck as a couple of the divers took his vest off. Then, before anyone could even yell a warning, a big wave came over the starboard side. It picked up the defenseless man, carried him across the deck, and slammed him into the bulkhead on the port side.

Opie now was badly hurt. Something had happened to his hip. He looked for someone to help him, but there was nobody nearby, so he crawled into the interior of the *Carolina* and into a cabin where Rozy sat propped up with his broken leg. When Tim Noble came down looking for him after a while, he found him curled up in a corner asleep.

By the time the *North Carolina* picked up Opie, it had gotten into shallow water and may even have hit bottom. However, if it did, the bottom was sandy and didn't seem to do much damage. Still, as quickly as possible, Richard got the *Carolina* back into deeper water and they went on searching.

The other two boats also continued to search, but they were finding fewer and fewer men. Occasionally there would be a tiny blinking light from a life vest, just a dot of light in a sea of darkness. But most often now, the light would be from an empty vest. The men on the ships would look and wonder if there ever had been a man in the life jacket and if so whether he was still alive. But never did they find a live person to accompany an empty floating jacket. They came across a few empty rafts too, but most of those had been blown far out of the search area. Some would be found in the following days washed up on beaches northeast of Carmen. Those few men who were picked up late that Sunday evening and who had been in the water the longest were often nearly unconscious, still breathing but unable to talk or to help themselves in any way. They were pulled from the water like sacks of rice. Often it took three or four men to get them on deck.

Richard Lobb, the barge superintendent, was dragged onto the *Ducker Tide* that night looking as if he might have suffered a heart attack. Since Shane Richins had just completed a first-aid course, he was called to look at the super and to administer CPR, if necessary. Shane determined that Lobb was just totally exhausted. He was put in the captain's cabin, and the next day the superintendent was walking around, smoking.

The last man the *Captain John* rescued was the 269's assistant captain, John Enriques, whom Tim Noble helped to leave the barge, then lost in the waves. Enriques had continued to drift by himself, helpless, and thinking for sure he would drown. He swallowed so much seawater, some mixed with oil, that at times he wished he *would* drown. But it seemed that whenever he'd given up all hope of being rescued and was ready to just sink beneath the waves, let death take him, he was shocked out of his misery by a more fundamental emotion—abject fear. Such powerful waves would loom over him that he thought they would drive him straight into the seabed.

So much time had passed that John felt it must be nearing morning. The seas covering him, and his existence in them, seemed endless, like a living nightmare that repeats and repeats the same agonies. The only way that maybe they would end was shortly, when his life would be snuffed in the waves. His semiconscious state was interrupted suddenly when from nowhere a searchlight hit him and then a boat was alongside and people were grabbing him.

Incoherent and totally incapable of helping himself, Enriques felt his body being hefted onboard. Kind hands tried to remove his life jacket, but he protested fiercely with his last ounce of strength: his life jacket was his savior and he needed it, could not give it up, refused to let it be taken off him. Still in his life jacket, he was carried into the crew's quarters, already filled with the injured. Space was found for him on the floor, along the wall, where he passed out.

John Enriques never was separated from his life jacket. Fortunately for him, he had been wearing a good one. Later it would become a prized possession. John eventually framed it, like a fine work of art, and mounted it on the wall of his office, where the jacket was a constant reminder of his surviving the worst that nature and life had ever put before him.

The three boat captains, each with a shipload of sick men, wondered at what point they should call off the search and head in to Carmen, the nearest port. The decision would soon be made for them, and it would nearly cost one of the captains his life.

Chapter Nine

❧

ROBERT TROSCLAIR had been controlling the tug from the doghouse, it seemed, as much as he had from the bridge. The doghouse was so small it was like sitting in a safety-glass-enclosed strait-jacket. Robert, 5 feet 11 inches and 180 pounds, was not an overly large man. Still, he just had room to sit in the operator's seat. Before him, on his left, were the engine and rudder controls. To his right were the controls for the towing cable drum, the anchor winch, and the floodlights and searchlights. The hydraulic and pneumatic hoses and the electric relays were all safely tucked away below the console, which housed all the instrument clusters.

Robert had finished in the doghouse and was leaving to return to the bridge. Enriques had conked out in a corner of a cabin. The crew and divers on the afterdeck had just gone below. There was no one to warn the captain that hurtling toward them from astern, and coming, it seemed, a mile a minute, was a rogue wave so large that it towered above the tug. And it was going to break right on top of them.

Robert neither saw the wave nor heard it over the roar of the storm. He had just left the doghouse when the wave hit, exploding the safety glass covering three sides and transforming it into a grenade of shards that blasted through the air. They demolished the seat Robert had just been sitting in and everything around it.

It is 25 feet from the doghouse to the side door of the wheelhouse. Maybe Robert sensed the wave behind him. There was nothing but a puny 3-foot-high railing around the boat deck, nothing that could prevent him from getting washed overboard right in front of his own tugboat—if he was lucky. If he was unfortunate, he would not clear the bow. On the main deck, 15 feet below, were the anchor windlass, the steel bitts around which line was wrapped, the bulwarks themselves; all these were in his path if the wave washed him off the bridge deck.

The door to the wheelhouse slides easily. Robert entered and was sliding the door shut when the wall of water hit. It knocked him into the stairwell that led up to the bridge. It put seawater down the stack, nearly killing the engines. If, even for a minute, the engines had shut down, the following wave would probably have capsized the tug. As it was, she rolled on her beam-ends, then righted herself. The wave also carried away the *Captain John*'s radar and her searchlight and knocked out her air-conditioning system. But it did not put the tug out of action and neither did it kill her captain or anyone else onboard.

At 2300 Harold Roche on the *Ducker Tide* and Trosclair on the tug decided to call off their search and try to get to a port. With the *Captain John*'s dog-house demolished, she could no longer safely pick up people. The vessels were also having trouble with dirt from the bottom of their fuel tanks clogging the fuel filters. Normally a certain amount of sediment settles and remains in the bottom of a ship's fuel tanks, and during regular sailing this is not a problem because the fuel lines leading to the engines are high enough off the tanks' bottoms that little or no sediment enters. But with the vessels' rolling and pitching, clogged fuel filters had become a major worry. One engine or the other on the vessels would suddenly shut down. Then the engineer would work furiously to change the filter and get the engine running again. Fortunately, on all three rescue boats this could be accomplished without shutting down the other, operating engine.

Most important, the three captains thought they had probably picked up nearly all the survivors they were going to find. The *North Carolina* had taken onboard fifty-four survivors. The *Ducker Tide* had rescued seventy-nine and the little *Captain John* had pulled in eighty-nine. The vessels had also fished out three bodies. The total accounted for most of the approximately 245 men on the 269—although at that point no one knew for sure exactly how many men had been onboard the barge when it sank.

There were other reasons to break off the search. The three vessels were filled to overflowing with injured, exhausted men. The interior decks were awash with vomit. Some of the men, perhaps because they had swallowed oil, had diarrhea and could not get to a head or found the few heads on the vessels already occupied. The ships still had to battle Roxanne's waves too, which were a constant threat, particularly if a mechanical breakdown occurred. Relatives on shore were clamoring to find out if their loved ones were alive. To reach port as soon as possible was now the captains' imperative.

When Kevin Dumont opened his eyes, he was still on the *Captain John*'s engine room grating. Lying next to him were two dead shipmates. Jim Vines, his head slumped on his chest, was crowded against Kevin. Angel, the radio operator, lay next to Vines. Every other inch of deck space was filled with survivors. Kevin could neither move nor tolerate the presence of the two dead men nearly on top of him. He again lapsed into unconsciousness.

Miguel Alvarez Cantu, the acting captain of the 269, had been brought aboard the *Captain John* earlier. Now he tried to make himself useful. He went around the tug with a pen and a pad identifying and listing those who had been rescued. Many of the barge's crew were in shock and could hardly remember their own names. Cantu was in shock as well. Still, he did his best. In the engine room, overflowing with survivors, he came across what he thought were three dead bodies: Angel, Jim, and Kevin. He noted the fact and dutifully went up to the bridge to report to the captain the identities of the three dead men. Robert Trosclair forwarded the names of the deceased over sideband to his office in Morgan City. Chuck Denning then passed the information on to McDermott headquarters and to the C.C.C. office in Ciudad del Carmen. The McDermott spokesman, wisely, gave out the names as *missing* until such time as their identities could be verified. Apparently C.C.C. did not provide any information about individuals to the public. In any case, Kevin's father and mother were told that their son was missing at sea.

According to Kevin, his father, an ex-barge superintendent, who probably had an inkling of the vulnerability of the 269, called the chief officers of J. Ray McDermott and said, "Listen, you sons of bitches, Kevin best not be missing." Kevin's mother, Erline Renois of Houma, Louisiana, heard of the sinking but was not sure that her son was on the barge. All night Sunday she and her family agonized. Then Monday morning she received a call from Gulf Technical Services, the company in Houston that had hired Kevin and other Americans on the barge crew to work for C.C.C. He *was* missing; her worst fears were confirmed. "You just never know what you are going to face when you wake up in the morning," she said later. "That's a terrible feeling, not knowing if [Kevin] was one of the survivors."

It wasn't until much later, when Kevin revived and had enough strength to wander up to the wheel-house, that anyone realized he *wasn't* dead. At that point a tired Robert Trosclair, still at the helm of the *Captain John* and battling the hurricane's seas, could do no more than exclaim over the fact. So for a long while the misunderstanding was not corrected. Chuck Rountree, Mitch Pheffer, and Phil Richard were also reported missing. Indeed, a McDermott spokesman drove out to Lafayette, Louisiana, to provide that misinformation to Katherine Richard, Phil's wife.

The tug's engine room, with the air conditioning destroyed, was almost unbearable. Victor Diaz, along with many others in the overcrowded tug, was forced to endure it. He had searched the vessel for a place to rest: "I finally managed to find a place to sit down," he recalled. "I saw one individual who was covered with a lot of vests, and I was thinkin', boy, you know, that's great. This guy's lucky. He can get some sleep. Come to find out there were more men being dragged in and they needed the space. The men started removing these vests, and it [the man underneath] happened to be Jim Vines. They took him out. I was right next to the exhaust and there was a lot of heat. There was a bucket that I was sittin' on. This bucket was against the exhaust and obviously it had a protective barrier, but it finally burnt through and the oil or grease, whatever it was, was falling on top of it and there was a small fire in the tugboat. It was put out by one of the guys that works on it. So I [went] down further below where the engines were, 'cause I wanted rest. I wanted to sleep and the only space was between these two huge engines. So I lay there and as the ship is being knocked around, they had a reservoir to collect any diesel and it swept [out of the reservoir] over the middle [between the engines] where my face was. It was hitting me so I could taste it. I finally got up and it was extremely loud. I made my way toward the garbage can and I found a piece of paper. It was full of grease. I didn't care. I threw it in my mouth. I took the grease out and I was chewing it. What I wanted to do was [get] some quiet. I cut it in half and shoved it in my ears and I went back and I laid down in the same spot where I was. [Eventually] I went back upstairs and I just sat there through the whole thing [the whole trip back]."

Ray Pepperday was also in the engine room. He remembered that the only place he could sit down was on the grating next to the dead men. "That was my first encounter with dead bodies—and I was 2 feet away staring into their dead eyes." Finally Ray got some plastic tarps, tied the bodies in them, and with some help from Kevin and others carried them outside and lashed them to the towing drum on the afterdeck.

Perhaps surprisingly, both the rescued and the rescuers said the trip back to Carmen in the over-crowded, storm-tossed vessels felt worse than anything else that night. Hurricane Roxanne had not abated nor had the size of the waves much decreased. By midnight Sunday the rescue vessels were still only

40 or 50 miles southeast of the hurricane's eye.
Roxanne started slowly moving west the next morning, but still at only a few miles an hour. The three
boats heading south-southwest for Carmen faced
20- to 25-foot seas now coming from all directions. It
was probably the worst for the smaller *Captain John*.
Seas continued to break on top of the pilothouse.
Robert Trosclair felt that any speed over 3 or 4 knots
would risk an oncoming wave's knocking out her
pilothouse windows. If that happened, the vessel's
remaining controls could quickly short out and the
tug would likely capsize.

The *Ducker Tide* preceded the other two vessels
toward port. Then came the *Captain John*. With no
radar, the tug depended on dead reckoning supplemented by positions radioed from the *North Carolina*
and later by course settings radioed from the Marine
Patrol Office in Carmen, which had the *Captain John*
on its radar. By the following morning they had only
made 14 miles of a 50-mile journey that in normal
sailing would take five or six hours.

On the *North Carolina* the situation was even
more precarious. Captain Richard Cassel had continued to look for survivors for about an hour after the
other two vessels had ended their searches and headed
for port. The *North Carolina* had not been able to find
anyone still in the water, so at about midnight she too

began the return trip home. She had been two hours on a heading of 225° when disaster hit.

Because of the pounding she was taking, slamming into wave after wave, the fuel line to her port engine vibrated so much it ruptured. Diesel sprayed around the engine room, smoking as it landed on engine blocks and especially on red-hot exhaust manifolds. Immediately the port engine was shut down.

Eulalio Zapata took the helm while Richard went down to consult with the engineer. Because the copper line had ruptured so badly and because fuel entering a marine diesel is under pressure, the break in the line couldn't be taped over as a temporary seal. Nor did the *Carolina* carry any spare fuel lines. So she resumed her journey on one engine. But since her remaining 2,000-hp EMD was capable of driving her at about 3 knots—the maximum speed she could make in the present weather conditions anyway—that in itself wasn't an insuperable problem.

Tim Noble spent much of the return trip in the *Carolina*'s wheelhouse. He and Richard had worked together for years. He watched as his friend nursed the *Carolina* toward port. Bleary-eyed from the better part of eighteen hours already spent at the helm, Richard now had to carefully ease his vessel over every crest and smooth her descent into every trough. The remaining engine had to be babied, protected as much as humanly possible, to prevent any kind of malfunction.

The fuel lines to the working engine were checked to make sure they weren't vibrating against anything. The biggest fear was not another break, however, but a clogged fuel filter. Previous to the rupture, one engine could be momentarily shut down while its fuel filter was changed. Now this was no longer possible. A clogged filter now would kill their remaining engine. If that happened, even briefly, the *Carolina* would go broadside to the waves and be knocked over. Without power to bring her back toward vertical and into the next wave, the *Carolina* and all the men onboard would likely be history. A sudden capsizing would put them in far more jeopardy than that faced by the men on the 269. So the few men in the pilothouse and in the engine room who knew the dangerous situation they were in held their breath as every wave hit the vessel. Hour after hour Cassel nursed the ship. Intermittently Zapata would take over the helm for thirty or forty minutes to give the captain a little relief. Even then, Richard wouldn't leave the bridge. Slowly they limped toward Carmen.

At 0530, just before dawn on Monday, October 16, Lt. Commander Jim Cullinan's Coast Guard C-130

Hercules had nearly reached the scene of the 269's last known location, about 70 miles due south of the hurricane's eye. He brought the plane in at about 10,000 feet, then began descending through Roxanne's eyewall. The ring of cumulonimbus clouds surrounding the hurricane's eye contained the fiercest winds. The C-130 bucked, leaped, dropped, and tossed from side to side as torrential sheets of rain pelted her. Nearing the eye, the altitude fluctuations intensified, sending them hurtling upward and then, like a roller coaster off its track, plunging into a stomach-churning free fall. With many other aircraft the pilot would have been worried, but not with the Hercules.

The C-130 Hercules, first produced by Lockheed Aircraft in 1954, is one of the most successful military transports ever built. Aside from its transport role it has been used by both the Coast Guard and the Air Force for search-and-rescue and weather reconnaissance. Its four Allison turboprops provide a range of up to 4,700 miles. It is also a stable aircraft. Even though Roxanne was giving it a pounding, Cullinan was not concerned about the safety of his plane. He was somewhat concerned, however, about the well-being of his flight crew, most of whom were in the back of the aircraft throwing up.

Suddenly the turbulence disappeared. They were

in the eye and it was a majestic sight: above them nothing but blue sky and sun, as if they were a million miles from a storm. But surrounding this golden oasis that covered an area about 12 miles in diameter were solid phalanxes of clouds extending up more than 30,000 feet and down close to sea level. It was like being in the center of a great football stadium built entirely of clouds.

Cullinan spiraled his C-130 down through the eye, then at about 2,000 feet took it through the second eyewall. More turbulence. The plane's engines roared, filling the whole cabin with sound at close to 130 decibels. The crew could only communicate using the microphones they each wore along with their earphones.

At 200 feet Cullinan leveled the plane off and began his search pattern. Back and forth they went, covering the area surrounding the 269's radioed position and then heading as far east as the Yucatan coastline. In five hours of searching, the crew saw nothing except flotsam. No rafts, no swimmers, and, surprisingly, not the 269 itself, even though the crane's A-frame was still sticking high out of the water.

Shortly after 1100, Cullinan noticed that the plane's reduction-gearbox pressure was fluctuating severely. The C-130 has constant-speed propellers and uses a reduction gearbox to drive the plane's generators. According to Cullinan, the plane has had a history of oil-pressure problems in the gearbox, and the fluctuating pressure was a sign that this one was ready to blow. Cullinan immediately went to power, then brought his plane up to cruising altitude. He told the rescue coordinator in New Orleans of his problem and said he was having to abort his mission and head back to base. The coordinator had no other Coast Guard resources in the area, but there was an Air Force weather recon aircraft in the vicinity, and he asked for its help.

The 53rd Weather Reconnaissance Hurricane Hunters is an Air Force Reserve squadron, part of the 403rd Wing at Keesler Air Force Base in Biloxi, Mississippi. The 53rd tracks hurricanes day in and day out during hurricane season. It is the only U.S. military squadron with that assignment, and its service area ranges from the mid-Atlantic to the equator to Guam in the Pacific. The 53rd's aircraft had been shadowing Roxanne for nearly a week, transmitting data they collected to the National Hurricane Center in Miami. One of the 53rd's planes had been flying 130-mile-long sweeps of Roxanne since before dawn.

Maj. Valerie Schmid, a flight meteorologist and an Air Force weather officer, was in the cockpit at a computer taking data from sensors mounted near the nose of the lumbering WC-130. It was nearly noon when they received a SATCOM message from their base.

Lt. Scott Spitzer, the copilot, received the call. After conferring with Maj. Bruce Neely, the aircraft commander, he came on the intercom to Major Schmid. "Hey, Val, we've got a real-world situation here! A 400-foot barge has sunk at coords 19.21N, 91.17W. About 200 people have been rescued, but twenty-three are still missing. Coast Guard requests we keep an eye open for any rafts or possible survivors."

The message they received went on to include frequencies on which to contact the Coast Guard plane on station and finished, "Do what you can!" It was signed by Capt. Brian Letourneau, duty operations officer.

Shortly after receiving the first message, the 53rd's plane received a second message stating that the Coast Guard's rescue aircraft was going to have to break off operations because of mechanical problems. Would they take over? The copilot answered in the affirmative and they began to plan their new, unexpected operation.

Neely, the pilot, asked the navigator how long they could stay on station. Navigator Tommy Moffit, after consulting with M. Sgt. George Bradley, the flight engineer, determined that they had enough fuel for two-and-a-half hours of search-and-rescue ops before reaching the minimum fuel level needed to get them home. The navigator set up a search pattern and the copilot received clearance from Mexican authorities to expand their intrusion into Mexican airspace.

Major Neely brought the WC-130 down to a search altitude of 500 feet. Major Schmid left her seat on the flight deck to take up a position at one of the two scanner windows located one on each side of the waist. Lt. John Dodge, a second copilot, took the opposite window. The 53rd's WC-130 (the W standing for weather) had been a rescue aircraft in a prior existence, so it had scanner windows. Now, however, in place of life rafts next to the rear drop doors, it contained meteorological instruments, along with a big auxiliary fuel tank that took up most of the plane's belly. The weather instruments were not going to do much good if they spotted someone, but with the Coast Guard plane gone, they were the only rescue aircraft on station.

They had been flying a grid west of Campeche for only forty-five minutes and were near the Yucatan shoreline when they spotted a life raft. The pilot swung the WC-130 around and on the second pass an arm waved to them from inside the raft. The pilot dipped a wing to let the survivor know that he had been seen. Then they radioed the raft's coordinates, 20-45.52N by 90-50.61W, to the rescue coordinator at District 8 Command Center. The raft was so close to shore that with the prevailing wind it would probably wash up on the beach before any vessel could get to it.

The WC-130 resumed its search, but all the crew saw was debris and empty life rafts, mostly upside down. At 1420 Monday, owing to low fuel, they broke off their search and headed back to base. After their long search, the crew were jubilant that they had even seen a survivor. Another Hurricane Hunter from the 53rd picked up the search but saw no survivors. The search was called off on Tuesday after determining that there were no unaccounted-for crew members.

Meanwhile, the three rescue vessels still plunged through big seas as they slogged their way back to port. Onboard, the poor survivors continued to vomit whatever little had been passed around from the ships' galleys and to suffer from the vessels' pitching and rolling. Ray Pepperday, on the *Captain John*, which was packed like a sardine tin full of sick men, said that the trip back seemed endless. He had been temporarily deafened in one ear when he hit the water after jumping off the 269. Sick, dehydrated, and only semiconscious, he thought, deliriously, that

maybe he had died and that this was to be his personal hell for all eternity.

Also on the *Captain John* was Raul Salabania
Acosta, the valve technician. He was so afraid the tug
would capsize in the waves that he would not go
below, where he might be trapped. All the way back
to Carmen Raul perched on top of the pilothouse,
still in his life jacket, holding on to a stanchion to
which he had also tied himself, in case a big sea tried
to carry him off or he lost consciousness. Wave after
wave struck him. Numerous times he almost lost his
handhold when the tug rolled or was hit. He with-
stood hundreds of waves covering the whole vessel.
He saw water pour down the stack and anxiously
heard the engines cough and sputter. For sixteen long
hours he endured the ordeal, with only one or two
others lashed alongside him. Still, he would not go
below.

The *Captain John*'s crew did what they could for
the survivors. Robert Trosclair and his men cleaned
out their lockers, giving away their extra clothes,
shoes, and whatever else they had. The galley was
also cleaned out of just about anything that could be
consumed without elaborate preparation. The boat
was still being thrown around so much that cooking
was out of the question. The sick men were everywhere, filling all the bunks, in every cabin, on every

inch of floor, and even strewn around the wheel-house, to the point where Trosclair and the mate had to tiptoe across the bodies to get from one side of the bridge to the other. Inside the tug, with no air condi-tioning, temperatures reached 120 degrees, so the men also had to endure stifling heat.

The situation on the other two boats wasn't much better. Though their air systems were operative and they were larger than the tug, they were still tak-ing a beating from the hurricane. Sometimes they were thrown into troughs until their props came out of water. Then the throttles would have to quickly be feathered before the overrides killed the engines. The captains, and the mates who sometimes spelled them at the controls, were all scared of that possibility. As Lorenzo Wilson, first mate of the *Captain John*, said, "In that kind of weather you can't afford to have the engines stall on you. If the engines stall at any moment I think the whole *Captain John* would be lost. The seas were so big that if those engines would have stalled it would have been a different story."

The *Ducker Tide*, with no major damage and running on both engines, was making a little better time than the other two. Still, her trip back to Carmen was miserable. Nearly everyone onboard was seasick. Lee Lloyd remembered, "It was the shittiest weather I've ever seen. Oh, man, God, it was just horrific! The waves were just hitting the boat, shaking it. I was concerned about us making it back. I've been sick before at sea, but never like this. I was up in the area behind the wheelhouse and I thought, well, maybe if I go down farther below I might find a lower center of gravity. I went down to the galley and opened the door from the stairway. The floor's covered with vomit. There's probably sixty guys lying there. Also, a dead guy with a sheet over him. Then right beside him they got people just laying there, right beside the dead guy. I said, 'Nooo, I don't believe I can stand this.'"

Lee, throwing up for most of the trip back, added, "It was one of those things, you know, where you're afraid that you'll die, then you're afraid you won't." Eventually he found himself a spot below where, along with all the others, he toughed it out the rest of the way.

Most of the men on the *Ducker* were as bad off as Lee, but a couple of them lucked out. Marco Polo, the diver, and a friend were starved. Neither had eaten anything in nearly twenty-four hours. The little food onboard had been distributed to the survivors, but for some reason Marco and his buddy hadn't received any. Now they rummaged around below deck searching for anything they could eat. They stumbled into the pantry, but it had already been cleaned out. Only one large jar remained untouched. They proceeded to gorge themselves on its contents. Although it was difficult to eat on the rolling, pitching ship, when they came out of the pantry after half an hour, they had satisfied smiles on faces covered with honey.

Back in Morgan City, Chuck Denning still maintained his radio vigil in North Bank Towing's office. He had been in contact with Robert Trosclair on the *Captain John* sporadically since the rescue began, but mostly Robert was too busy to carry on much of a conversation—not that he was talkative at the best of times. Robert had periodically radioed the number of survivors he had picked up. After pulling in as many people as he could find near the 269, he and the other captains swept northeast following the prevailing wind and seas. Robert had given Chuck his approximate position, and Chuck had told him about how much farther he could safely go before the water became too shallow, verifying Robert's position and fathometer readings. With the waves hitting the ship, going aground was too risky to contemplate.

As the evening wore on, more demands were made on Chuck from McDermott executives and others who had heard about the sinking and required information about individuals who had been on the barge. McDermott wanted the names of their employees who were onboard the three rescue vessels to provide to the men's families who were beseeching them. This information was not easy to come by. The rescue crews were too busy spotting and pulling people out of the water to go around and get everyone's names, and most of the survivors were too exhausted to make a list of names. On the *Captain John* one survivor, John Wheeler, a life-support tech, worked with Miguel Alvarez Cantu to compile a list of everyone rescued. John had also helped on deck to pull people aboard.

Chuck Denning had been joined the previous afternoon by Captain Hans Fuhri, McDermott's Gulf marine superintendent, who lived close by. Captain Fuhri acted as a liaison between his superiors and the men on the vessels. He stayed with Chuck until 0100 Monday morning relaying information as it came from the *Captain John* and the *North Carolina*. Some information about the situation on the *Ducker Tide* also was passed on by Captain Robert.

When the three captains called off the search, they decided to head for Carmen because it was the closest port. The next safe harbor was Dos Bocas, but that was an additional 50 miles into the teeth of the hurricane. At the 3 knots they were making, sailing there would have taken another twelve to sixteen hours. With three boatloads of sick and injured men, they considered that option unacceptable. But going into Carmen did have some drawbacks. As was noted earlier, the channel leading in to Carmen's sheltered lagoon was shallow and poorly marked. There were no channel buoys, just range lights. Also, certain points in the channel sometimes had only 14 feet of water. For these reasons, Chuck Denning had urged his two captains not to risk the channel in storm conditions but to head for Dos Bocas instead. Tidewater's area manager urged Harold Roche on the *Ducker Tide* to do the same. The *Captain John* drew 14 feet, the *North Carolina* a little more, and the *Ducker Tide*, the deepest-draft towing vessel Tidewater operated in the area, had a 17-foot draft.

While the vessel owners and, in the case of the *North Carolina*, the charterer might have wanted their vessels to head for the safer port, the final decision rested with the captains. On all three vessels the captains felt they needed to risk the channel into Carmen, so they continued in that direction.

James J. Riddle, McDermott's diving safety officer, was just getting out of bed on Monday morning, October 16, when he received a phone call from Mike Ambrose informing him of the 269's sinking. J. J. was stunned. When he had left work on Friday, everything seemed OK. The first question on his mind was whether the diving crew had been rescued and whether they were all right. From information passed on to Chuck Denning during the night, he learned that three divers were still not accounted for, and some others were injured. Then J. J. asked to go to Carmen to help out. His request was granted. He threw some clothes into a suitcase, had his wife call the local bank manager at home to get him some money, and headed out.

The dive crew on the 269 were not just employees to J. J. Many of them were friends—and some of them were his best friends. Over the years he had worked closely with Chuck Rountree, Tim Noble, and Roy Cline. In fact, Roy Cline's Toyota 4 Runner was sitting in J. J.'s front yard, where Roy had left it for safekeeping when he went to work on the barge. After stopping at the bank and the office, J. J. set out in Roy's Toyota, figuring to leave it for him at the New Orleans airport.

Highway 90 runs the 85 miles between Morgan City and New Orleans International, where J. J.'s wife had booked him a flight to Mexico City. He would figure a way to get to Carmen once he arrived in Mexico. However, problems seem to beget problems. Halfway to New Orleans the Toyota's engine blew. The camshaft had seized. J. J. remembers being stuck out in the middle of the rice fields, so upset that he was on the verge of tears.

Eventually he did get to the airport and found his ticket waiting for him. After arriving in Mexico City he went to McDermott's office there and introduced himself to Mike Lamm, president and C.E.O. of McDermott International, who happened to have been in the Mexico City office prior to the sinking. Lamm told him, "You need to get down there and see what you can do. I got a plane out there," he added. "Take it." The plane was a six-passenger executive jet. J. J. took it and headed for Carmen.

At 1600 on the sixteenth, the *Captain John* surfed her way through the Carmen channel guided by the *Seabulk Austin*, which had come out of the bay to assist her. The *Ducker Tide* had arrived three hours earlier. The *North Carolina*, running on only one engine and remaining to look for more survivors, wouldn't get in for another four hours. Luckily the vessels did not go aground in the shallow channel, likely because of the 5-foot storm surge that was a product of Roxanne's winds actually raising the level of the sea. That same surge flooded the entire town of Carmen, which had 4 feet of standing water and rivers running through the main streets.

By 1700 the *Captain John* had secured to the barge *Sara Maria* to offload her eighty-nine survivors.

The *Ducker Tide* had put her survivors on the *Sara Maria* earlier, where they were met by doctors, nurses, food, and fresh water. The *Sara Maria* had sufficient quarters for everyone, and after the survivors were fed and showered they were able to climb into clean bunks for some badly needed sleep.

The crew of the *Captain John* had one more chore. At 1815 they secured their vessel to the Pemex dock, where they delivered the two bodies they had taken from the sea as well as the one the *Ducker Tide* had had onboard. Then Captain Trosclair and his crew grabbed what food they could from the depleted icebox and crashed in their bunks.

The Yucatan Peninsula had experienced one of the worst hurricane seasons in history. Between September 15 and October 16 four hurricanes (Iris, Opal, Roxanne, and Roxanne again) had hit the area, killing dozens and leaving some 160,000 people homeless. Besides Carmen, nearly all the other coastal towns and cities were flooded.

Six people died during Roxanne in addition to those who died in the 269 sinking. Two of the six went down in a small sailboat that capsized. Roxanne nearly drove the *Patriot*, a 95,000-deadweight-ton Liberian tanker owned by Conoco (Oil) Shipping Company, aground on the north side of the Yucatan near Campeche. It also turned a Carnival cruise into a Carnival nightmare for the passengers on the *Carnival Tropicale* as it sailed near Cozumel. Most of the *Tropicale*'s 600 passengers, who had experienced unremitting seasickness and fear, signed a petition demanding a full refund. Carnival gave the passengers a forty-dollar shipboard credit each and discount certificates for future cruises.

By the time J. J. Riddle arrived in Carmen that Monday evening, most of the survivors had just gotten in and had showered and eaten. Delighted to see them alive, he went up and hugged his friends and even kissed some of them. Their delight, to be sure, was every bit as great as his. The survivors badly needed dry clothes to replace their sodden, oil-covered shirts and pants. The company had made a substantial effort to provide clothes, to the point of buying out Carmen's small department store's entire stock of men's garments. These were supplemented by C.C.C. guard uniforms and even old cooks' whites. Those in the whites looked like they were part of the Army medical team that had set up an emergency receiving station in some offices on the barge's deck, where they administered to the injured.

The next morning was Tuesday, October 17. Roxanne was again heading north—away from Carmen, away from the Yucatan, and away from the 269's crew. Ray Pepperday remembers that he hadn't been able to sleep that night, so early, at about 0600, he got up and went outside. "I get out there," he says, "and the sun's just starting to rise. It's already cleared up and it's going to be a beautiful day. Shane Richins was standing there and I told him that I really wondered if I was going to see the light of day one more time. He didn't have a lot to say; he just basically nodded in agreement. And we stood there and watched the sun rise."

❧

B Y MONDAY MORNING the day following the sinking, there were officially twenty-three men dead or missing. Three of the dead would be brought in by the rescue vessels. Two more would later be found floating in the warm Gulf waters, bloated, and partially eaten by passing fish. Three bodies would never be found, and those men would be presumed dead. Included in this category was the man in the raft spotted by the Hurricane Hunters, who apparently never made it to shore. Fifteen of the missing, however, had never left the sunken barge. One of those was Luis Domingo, the teenage *manio-brista*.

Sunday afternoon, alone on the heliodeck, Luis watched the last few men flee the sinking vessel. As much as he wished to join them, he was so scared of leaping into the mountainous waves that his muscles seemed paralyzed. So all he could do was watch as the sea came closer and closer to engulfing him. Then, from somewhere, he thought he heard people calling. That was impossible. There was no one else on deck. But he heard it again and, turning, glanced up into the air behind him. Nothing was left but the remains of the crane.

Before the hurricane had even hit, the 275-foot-long boom of the big crane had been secured for bad weather in its steel crutch welded to the foredeck. Two shipping containers used for storage had also been secured forward, but waves sweeping the 269 had torn them from their lashings and sent them careening crazily around the deck. Almost immediately they were washed over the side, but one, on its haphazard journey, first smashed into the big crane's boom crutch. Subsequently, the boom was pushed into the air by waves rolling underneath it. As the 269's stern settled farther and farther into the sea, the boom, still supported by the steel cables attached to it, began rising. Some crew members who had been on the crane scrambled onto the boom itself, but as waves began hitting it, they climbed up on the massive A-frame that rose nearly 80 feet above the top of the crane body. The A-frame looked like an open stepladder with two legs mounted on top of the crane body and the other two hinged to the base of the boom. Steel cables ran from the end of the boom to drums on top of the A-frame, and when these were winched in or out, the boom was raised or lowered. The men who had been calling Luis were scattered up the latticed section of the A-frame connected to the boom. They looked as though they were clinging to a ladder jutting from the ocean floor. They waved for him to join them.

Luis's body parts suddenly came to life. He scrambled down the ladder to the walkway around the crane, then up the ladder to the top of the crane, and finally, more nervously, up the steel lattice of the A-frame. It had ladders running up it at a 45-degree angle, so normally it would not have been too difficult to climb. However, with the 269 rocking as each wave hit, and being pelted by blown spray and rain, Luis climbed slowly and fearfully. When he reached the first clump of men high up the lattice, he stopped and tied himself to a cross-brace with a piece of rope that he had picked up on deck. Then he had a chance to get his bearings.

Some of the fourteen other men were on the A-frame. Others were on a narrow platform at the top. Luis did not know any of the men, though he recognized most of them. All but one had used pieces of rope to tie themselves to cross-members. Strangely, the one person who had no rope to make a safety line for himself was the crane operator. An older man, heavyset, he had worked with Luis nearly every day, yet they had never spoken to each other because this man sat high in the crane's cab. The fellow was wedged into a V formed by the lattice 20 or 30 feet above Luis's head. Eventually someone cut off a piece of his own safety line and gave it to the crane operator so that he too would have a rope to stop him from falling in case he slipped.

Within an hour from the time Luis joined the others, it got dark. He had hoped that one of the rescue vessels would come over and pick them up, but none of them were close by. The lights from the three vessels were visible far to the southeast, for this was the direction that most of the survivors had drifted. Except for the A-frame, the 269 now was totally submerged. If the rest of the 269's crew had known that the A-frame would remain above the surface, more of them would certainly have opted to join the survivors there rather than taking their chances in the sea.

Waves seemed to be coming dangerously close to where Luis and some of the others sat, trying to hunker down on the steel beams and to face away from the driving rain. One by one the men began climbing higher on the A-frame to avoid spray from the wave crests. As air escaped from various compartments below deck, the barge settled onto the ocean floor. She was in about 60 feet of water, enough to cover the crane cab once her hull sank into the sand-and-mud bottom. Thirty-five- and sometimes 40-foot waves would thunder below the men clinging like limpets to the steel framework that was their only salvation. The top of the A-frame was 155 feet above the bottom of the 269's keel, so the stranded men could avoid even the largest waves, but not the spray or the rain or the wind, which tore at them, driving salt into their eyes and skin. Since the men on the platform seemed to be more vulnerable, a few climbed down and tied themselves to beams below the platform.

Through the night the fifteen men kept watch, hoping they would see one of the vessels' lights coming closer, and a few times a ship did come nearer, but never close enough for the ship's crew to see them. They waved frantically whenever a vessel got at all close, but the big spotlights never more than briefly flashed in their direction. With the poor visibility, the tug and the supply boats would have had to come pretty close before the men could be seen—and that never happened. Late in the night as the men looked toward the southeast, all the lights had disappeared. They were truly alone.

Luis huddled with four other men three-quarters

of the way up the A-frame. One fellow was about 10 feet below them, and the other nine were mostly in small groups above them or on the platform. As the night wore on, the men got colder and colder. They tried crouching together to get a little warmth, but beyond giving each other some reassurance that they weren't alone, this seemed to do little good. Many of them feared that if they fell asleep they would lose their grip and that their safety lines, simply old bits of manila cordage, would unravel or break. In some cases two men had shared a piece of rope by dividing the strands, and they were particularly worried. Luis and an older fellow next to him woke each other when either of them slumped into unconsciousness. The agony of trying to stay awake all the time added considerably to the litany of their miseries—cold, hunger, aches, salt-stung eyes, and open cuts.

Finally, dawn came and revealed an empty sea. Not a ship, not a plane. Well, soon there would be a rescue boat for them, right? Their bosses had to know there were so many of them missing, yes? The older crewman next to Luis, a man from Tuxla, tried to reassure him. Luis felt a fear and a despair that he had never known. He didn't think that he could hang on much longer. He and all the others kept moving and changing positions slightly to ease cramped and sore muscles and to spread the pain of the particular part of an arm or leg that was pressed into or over a steel girder. But nothing they could do really gave them any relief.

Shortly after dawn they heard a plane. Fifteen faces scanned the skies for their rescuer. Then to the east they saw it, a big, fat-bodied, four-engine patrol plane. One guy thought it was the Mexican Air Force. Another said no, it was the American Coast Guard, and sure enough, someone else said they could see a star on it—so it had to be the Coast Guard. It was patrolling back and forth only a few hundred feet above the water. Obviously it was looking for them. Soon it would see them and they would be rescued and there would be food and hot coffee and beds and warmth. Their spirits rose.

But the plane the stranded men saw was not the Coast Guard's C-130 Hercules; it was the Air Force's Hurricane Hunter. The Coast Guard C-130, with gearbox problems, had already headed back to base, having found nothing but empty life rafts and debris. Its crew had somehow missed seeing the fifteen survivors clinging to the crane's A-frame.

The men watched the patrol plane make low sweeps, but after they first saw it, it never again came close to them. Then, after a while, they didn't even hear the engines. That was when Luis became frantic. They would never be found. He and the other men had been praying off and on through the night. Now they began praying once more. Luis felt terror well up within him. He thought of his family. He would never see them again. He began to cry and he couldn't stop crying. The older men in his group tried to comfort him. "Don't worry," they yelled to him above the wind. "We will be found. Trust in God. We will be rescued." Their words didn't do much good. Luis was sure he was going to die.

As Monday dragged on, more of the men began to lose hope. The afternoon provoked thoughts about another miserable night on the A-frame. Also they were hungry and thirsty. The lack of water was the worst. Luis and the guy next to him huddled with his windbreaker cupped between them to catch rainwater. The little they managed to collect they eagerly gulped down. Somebody had the cap of an asthma inhaler. They filled it and passed a little water to some of the others who had no means of collecting their own and who were begging them for a drink.

Since they had eaten nothing, they had no need to defecate, but urinating was a problem. Whoever needed to urinate first had to untie himself and work his way down below the others so that the wind wouldn't blow it all over them. Climbing down, holding a beam while they urinated, and then climbing back up to their perch was dangerous because they were so weak and stiff. It would be only too easy to lose your footing or your grip and go crashing into the sea. Fortunately, everyone managed to do it without incident.

Sometime in the midafternoon, they heard a helicopter. After a few minutes it appeared, a beautiful blue whirlybird circling right above them. The blond gringo pilot was waving at them. Every man on the boom, no matter how weak, waved back. They were found! They were saved! The helicopter circled a few more times and then sped away. They scanned the horizon for the ships that certainly would have been alerted and that must at this very instant be speeding toward them. But no ships appeared. They looked and looked, they prayed and looked. Then it began to get dark, and their hopes faded with the light.

The second night was even worse. The wind and seas had moderated a bit, but the men were so much weaker that every movement was torture. Yet not moving, getting locked into one position, made muscles cramp fiercely. Some of the men, Luis included, didn't think they would last until dawn. Luis's teeth were chattering uncontrollably and he felt sick. He hadn't eaten in nearly two days. The old line tying him to the steel beam cut into his gut, but if it parted he was a goner. Yet despite his fears, his shaking, and his nausea, Luis kept falling asleep. Sometimes he caught himself. Sometimes the older comrade next to him, a kitchen worker, shook him awake. Somehow the night passed.

The *Sara Maria* still hummed with activity Tuesday morning. The barge had been towed in through the narrow channel just prior to Roxanne's second appearance. With the aid of the storm surge it had gotten nearly a quarter mile before it grounded. And there it sat on one side of the narrow passage, with a bevy of small boats coming and going around it. As each of the three rescue vessels finally made it to port, they tied up to the *Sara Maria*.

At 1700 on Monday the sixteenth, when the *Captain John* had arrived and slid alongside, even before the tug was secured to the barge, one of the first people Kevin Dumont saw was Richard Lobb, who was standing by to greet the survivors with a big smile on his face. "We made CNN, Kevin. We made CNN!" he shouted.

Kevin pointed to the two shrouded corpses lying on the deck and replied, "No, y'all didn't make CNN. That's what y'all made," and marched off the tug.

The first thing Kevin did on reaching the *Sara Maria* was to phone his mother. Erline later said, "I was in tears, in hysterics. I was so happy I was crying." Kevin told her, "I'm OK. I'm all in one piece. I'm fine. Mom, don't do this to me. Don't cry or you'll get me crying too."

Lenn Cobb phoned his wife, Noni, in Alabama Monday night. Noni and their fourteen-year-old son, Dusty, had been riveted to the Weather Channel for days watching Roxanne's original course across the Yucatan, knowing that Lenn and the others on the 269 were right in its path. "It's time we said a prayer for your father," she told Dusty. Then Roxanne moved on, and she didn't give it another thought. She went to Atlanta on Sunday for the christening of Lenn's grandnephew and returned home Monday to find two close friends waiting for her. One friend had talked to a McDermott representative who had told her the hurricane had swung back around and had sunk the 269, but Lenn was safe. Noni didn't believe he was alive, wouldn't believe it until she heard Lenn's voice. Dusty, on the other hand, was confident that his dad had made it through and was OK. Noni suffered all that afternoon and evening until Lenn's call put her mind at rest. The other families suffered as well until one by one the survivors reported in.

Tuesday the barge's main deck looked like a three-ring circus without the animals. Men in a dramatic array of attire strolled back and forth. Sport jackets were mismatched with guards' uniform bottoms, slacks paired with starched white cooks' shirts, and shorts joined dress shirts three sizes too large or too small for their wearers. In the grab bag following the rescue boats' arrivals, no one seemed to have been able to snatch off the pile both what fit him and what matched anything else.

One of the mismatched was Ray Pepperday. On his promenade around the deck in an oversize pair of parachute pants and a child's shirt that he couldn't button, he glanced up as he passed the makeshift hospital. Standing in front of it was the foreman whose arm he had freed from the steel door. In spite of his sling-bound arm, upon seeing Ray he gave his rescuer a smile from ear to ear.

Onboard the *Sara Maria*, some of the dive crew met on deck. Once they had voiced their individual joys over still being alive, their conversation turned to their sorrow over the loss of Jim Vines. The divers who had been with him felt terrible, as though they should have taken better care of him.

"Seeing Jim's body float by hit me like a hammer," Lenn Cobb said. Lee Lloyd added, "The last time I saw him he was back on deck taking off his boots. That's the last time I saw him. He was scared to death. If we'd only known how scared he was, that he wasn't going to jump, we would have pushed him in front of us." They all agreed that if they had been aware of how afraid Jim was, they could have saved him. Mitch Pheffer and Phil Richard, the two young divers, were especially distraught. Just as they were ready to jump off the starboard bow, which was then almost in the sea, Jim had come up to them and warned them against jumping there—that he had seen men get swept under the barge who had gone in from that location. So, along with Jim, they had moved over to the high side. He had asked for their help, as he had the others, and they had assured him they would take care of him in the water. It was Phil and Mitch who had retrieved his body and brought it aboard the *Captain John*. "I feel like we failed him," Mitch said later, "and he was the one guy who had gone out of his way to help us."

Later, Lee reflected on the situation again. "I've thought about it a lot. I agonized over it for a long time. It bothered me—it still bothers me that I didn't just grab the guy and just physically [take care of him]. One of us would have gotten on one side and one on the other, but we just didn't know." As in war, the self-recriminations for having failed to save a doomed comrade follow the survivors, in this case for years.

The makeshift hospital was rapidly running out of patients. Nine or ten men had broken arms, legs, fingers, or toes. All but the toes had been placed in casts or splints. Men with lesser injuries, mostly contusions and abrasions, who had not been seen the previous evening were presently being treated. All the men, with or without injuries, now wanted only one thing: to get home as soon as possible. Strangely, however, they found they were not permitted to leave the barge.

The 269 was McDermott's second barge to sink with loss of life in just four years. C.C.C., which had direct responsibility for the barge's safety, was also sensitive to bad publicity. Already the phone lines of both companies were jammed with newsmen wanting not just information but, more important, interviews with the survivors. Reporters had also gathered in Ciudad del Carmen and were attempting to get out to the *Sara Maria*. It seems that they were denied access to the barge, and the Mexican survivors, with few exceptions, were not permitted ashore. According to Lee Lloyd and Kevin Dumont, the Americans were told not to talk to reporters—in fact, to anyone. Bland press releases giving the briefest recounting of the sinking and current figures on the dead and missing were about all that was offered by the companies. Perhaps officials of the companies thought that the whole episode would blow over quickly if the newspapers had little to report; if so, they were correct. News of the tragedy made headlines in Mexico for only a few days. In the United States some newspapers, mostly ones in whose territory individual American survivors lived, gave the story greater play once they interviewed those who returned. For the most part, however, American news coverage was also cursory and brief.

On Wednesday morning eighteen of the American dive staff left on a commercial flight booked by J. J. and Ed Burgueno, McDermott's diving rep in Carmen. Ron Rozmarynoski, with his broken leg in a cast, and John Wheeler departed later that day on McDermott's private jet. Also along was J. J., who carried a nearly empty suitcase onboard, having given almost all his spare clothes to the dive crew.

Most of the Mexican crew, after being forced to stay on the *Sara Maria* for two days, were finally given their back pay and allowed to go home. The morning after their arrival, Gustavo Zaldivar, the storesman, had asked to go home. According to Gustavo, one of the managers told him, "No, you don't have to go. You can't go." Gustavo replied, "I have to. I have to see my family." He subsequently ignored the order and took a boat carrying the injured to shore. His wife of thirty years was surprised when he walked in the house. Somehow she had not heard about the sinking.

Carmen is a small place, however, and word travels fast. Most of the other wives and families had knowledge of the 269's sinking by the morning following the incident. Churches began to fill as worried families went to pray for their loved ones. No list of the survivors had been released, so families didn't know if their men were alive or dead. Raul Salabania Acosta's wife, Bruna, remembers that she was praying that her husband was alive. She began crying as she prayed. Then the phone rang. Fearfully she picked it up. Raul said, "I'm fine. Don't worry about me. I love you and I'll be home soon."

On the *Sara Maria,* after food, a shower, and fresh clothes, Marco Polo found himself in the middle of a crying, laughing throng, congratulating themselves on coming through alive. "We made it! We did it!" they said, hugging each other through tears of joy. Marco himself felt that they had done something big, just by coming through. "I felt so happy," he said, "because I never thought I was going to survive."

Marco was worried that his mother, who had a serious heart condition, would think he had been lost in the sinking. "There was another guy by the name of Leopoldo," he said. "He worked for Pemex certifying the work we were doing. They called him 'Polo,' the same as me. They found him dead, floating in the water with his face down. So if my mother hears that this guy Polo is dead, she's going to think 'Ay' it's me." As it turned out, however, Marco's mother hadn't even known her son was on the sunken barge.

Eventually, when the workers were allowed to return to their families, Marco went to his mother's house. Walking in the door, he pretended at first that nothing had happened. Only when she noticed his new ill-fitting clothes did the story slowly, hesitantly, come out, and by that time there was no need to worry.

Far out in the Gulf, those men still on the A-frame of the sunken 269 could not believe that nobody had yet come to save them. With dawn on Wednesday, their hopes rose again. Surely a boat would come today. About midmorning, there was a shout from men high up on the platform. Then the other men saw them. Masts on the horizon were rising and sinking behind wave crests. In an hour, three vessels—two supply boats and a Mexican Navy patrol craft—lay on each side of the sunken 269. A sailor with a bullhorn called to the men to climb down and swim to the boats. The captains were afraid to bring their vessels too close for fear of damaging their props on underwater parts of the 269 protruding near the surface.

Along with the others, Luis untied his rope and carefully worked his way down the ladders. Neither he nor the other men had any strength left, and they were all afraid they would fall as they clumsily descended. But they all made it to within 10 or 15 feet of the water. Then one after another they jumped and swam to one of the boats rocking in the swells.

The waves now were only 6 or 8 feet high, but still Luis had trouble paddling the 50 or 60 feet to the nearest vessel. As the supply boat rolled toward him, strong hands grabbed his life vest and yanked him onboard the *Isla del Cedros*. On deck he stood shaking and wavering. One of the crew said, "Go on inside. Can you do that?" Luis replied, "I don't know." He took a couple of steps toward the deckhouse before he lost consciousness.

He awoke on a bunk in one of the utilitarian, Formica-lined cabins. He thought the crew would give him food and dry clothes, but he says they told him he'd have to wait until they got into Carmen, where C.C.C. would have food and clothes for him. When the *Isla del Cedros* and the other two boats docked in the commercial boat harbor that afternoon, Luis and the others went into C.C.C's offices nearby. It was as if they had not even been on the 269. According to Luis, they were given neither welcome nor food nor clothing, nothing but their back wages— and good-bye. With some of his earnings Luis bought food from a sidewalk vendor and gobbled it down. Then he walked slowly home to his uncle's house on a Carmen back street.

❧

Chapter Eleven

A STORM OF litigation has followed the 269 sinking. Nearly all the Mexican and most of the American crew members sued C.C.C. and its parent corporations, C.F.C. and J. Ray McDermott, accusing the companies of operating an unsafe vessel and of needlessly risking their lives. The companies have denied any wrongdoing. However, before asking who is to blame—and certainly there are plenty of accusations to go around—the first question is why the tragedy occurred in the first place. The decision makers were intimately familiar with sea conditions in the area and with the effects of hurricanes, having decades of experience with both in this particular oil patch.

Richard Lobb had been the 269's superintendent on and off since 1972 and had been working in the Gulf of Mexico for at least ten years prior to the sinking. Joe Perot, Lobb's superior and operations manager, had previously worked for Brown and Root for thirty-one years. During much of that time he was in charge of area operations, directing work and equipment, much as he did for C.C.C. There is no question that the two men knew their jobs, knew the condition of the 269, and knew the area in which they were working. Why didn't they move the 269 out of the path of the hurricane? Why did the barge sink and what could have been done to prevent it?

Obviously, if the 269 had followed the *Sara Maria* and the *Mega Dos* into the sheltered bay at Carmen, eight lives and untold amounts of misery would probably have been saved. Even starting as late as Saturday evening at, say, 2200, there would have been time to tow the barge into Carmen or Dos Bocas and maybe into Coatzacoalcos, though that port was 160 miles from the 269's position, and even towing at 3 ½ knots it would have taken the better part of two days to get there. Since Coatzacoalcos was farther from Roxanne's track, however, the sailing might have been easier and faster.

Another possibility, once the decision had been made to face Roxanne at sea, would have been to take excess crew members off the 269 using crew boats, leaving just enough men to repair towlines and handle the anchors. Having crew boats remove men certainly would have been feasible prior to Roxanne's first visit. By October 14, however, when it was first realized that Roxanne might be heading back toward the barge, conditions were probably already too rough to permit transferring crew to smaller boats. Generally, it's too dangerous for men to be transferred in waves of more than 8 to 10 feet, and already Saturday evening the vessels were plowing through waves 12 to 14 feet high. Neither was using helicopters an option at that point. According to officials at Heliservicio Campeche, S.A., the helicopters in the area in 1995 could not operate in winds over 50 to 55 knots (57 to 61 mph). By dawn Sunday the winds far exceeded those limits.

What about just beaching the 269 northeast of Carmen? The captains of two smaller self-propelled barges certainly considered that choice Sunday morning as Roxanne headed back toward them. But it seems likely that Richard Lobb made the correct decision not to attempt beaching his barge. The area between Carmen and Campeche, 110 miles to the northeast, was the most probable location for such a beaching. North of Campeche the tidelands shoal out some 15 miles, and the 269 would have been stranded where no one could easily reach shore. Even south of Campeche the 269 could not have gotten closer than a quarter mile from the beach before grounding. If she were aground that far from shore with 40-foot waves pounding her, she could well have broken up, as Lobb predicted she would be. The men would have been forced into a monstrous surf littered with flotsam from the barge, and the death toll could have been much higher than it was.

The two other options were to tow the 269 to another location where she might ride out the hurricane or to try to hold position just east of the oil field, which is the decision that was made both times Roxanne approached. Evidently little or no thought was given Saturday evening, October 14, to towing the barge 25 miles due north, where the water depth is at least 130 feet instead of the 70 to 80 feet in which she tried to survive Roxanne. According to Richard Lobb's testimony in a deposition, it was decided to tow the 269 to shallower water, 15 to 20 miles southeast of the Nohoch-A platform, where it might be calmer. In fact the area to which the 269 was towed was a "cleared towing area" and a preferred location for riding out storms, Lobb said.

Hendrik Tolman, a Dutch civil engineer and mathematician, is one of the world's foremost experts on wave structure. He trained in coastal engineering and the subcategory of offshore engineering at

Holland's Delft University. He specialized in design-
ing and analyzing structures that are erected in the
surf zone. He now works as a contractor for the
National Center for Environmental Prediction in
Camp Springs, Maryland. Hendrik makes estimates
of wave size, which the center then uses as part of
storm warnings for mariners.

Upon analyzing the 269's positions on the fifteenth, the water depths involved, and Roxanne's
positions relative to the barge, Tolman was not at all
surprised that she sank. "This thing [the 269] basically ran into the surf zone," he said. "They really got
nailed because they were simply in too shallow water.
And they went really, basically, from the perspective
of how waves transform, from being pretty bad in the
deep ocean [during a hurricane] to being absolutely
horrendous entering the surf zone."

As the 269 and her tugs were driven east by
Roxanne's wind and waves, they sailed into even
shallower water until, where the 269 sank, it was only
50 to 60 feet—and they were still more than 30 miles
from shore. Nevertheless, the surf zone, according
to Tolman, is a function of the ratio between water
depth and wave height, rather than distance from
shore.

"The shallower it gets," Hendrik continued, "the
slower a wave can go forward, but it still has all

this energy to move forward, so it grows higher and steeper. If it gets too high, it cannot support the amount of energy that it transports. When that occurs, the crest of the wave goes faster than the wave itself and literally falls off. Then you get breaking waves. The highest individual waves you can have are about half the water depth, so if the barge was in 80- then 60-foot water depths, the waves were 25 or 35 and occasionally 40 feet. As soon as you get into the surf zone, you rapidly transition into a place where almost every other wave breaks [and] walls of water [hit] you continuously. So for practical purposes, they essentially went on the beach."

Hendrik further reflected on what might have saved the 269. "If they had managed to get themselves 25 miles to the north the day before, they might have been able to ride this thing out without trouble. They would have been uncomfortable, but they would not have been in the transition zone, where basically you are on the beach already." Thus it seems the choice of location for the 269 to ride out Roxanne may have contributed to her sinking.

In the litigation that followed the sinking of the 269, attorneys would also argue that some of the loss of life—and the trauma suffered by the survivors—was attributable to deficient lifesaving gear and lack of drills. According to several crew members interviewed, there were never any safety or lifeboat drills on the barge. So when she went down, they said, some people couldn't find their life jackets and many others who did find them didn't know how to wear them. Richard Lobb recalled only one lifesaving drill and could not remember when it occurred. If there had been regular drills, attorneys argued, everyone would have had a life jacket, would have known where it was, and would have known how to wear it. This was a double tragedy, since many of the crewmen did not know how to swim.

Then there are the questions raised about the number and quality of the jackets themselves. Richard Lobb said that all of the life preservers had been properly inspected prior to Roxanne. According to the testimony of several survivors, however, many were the original life jackets issued when the 269 was new, twenty-eight years before the sinking, still lettered with the 269's original name, *L. B. Meaders*. Some of the jackets didn't have lights, or at least ones that worked. Many men only had the flat work vests, which are not made to be worn for long periods in the water and do not have the buoyancy of regular life jackets. Even worse, some of the crewmen claimed, many of the vests and life jackets had deteriorated and should have been replaced. Acid and other corrosives spilled on some vests had dissolved the plastic foam flotation. Survivors said that many jackets had lost part of their flotation, and in some cases the jacket fabric was rotten. According to Eulalio Zapata, Pitalua Mazaba said part of the reason he lost all his front teeth was that he had exhausted himself swimming because his jacket didn't have enough flotation. Another crewman, fished naked out of the water by a rescue boat, said he had taken off his clothes because his life vest wouldn't support him and his clothes were dragging him down.

Angel Fernandez Ramirez, whose body was found in the sea near Mérida, was wearing a flat work vest, though it is not certain that he drowned. One fatality may be linked to a worn-out jacket. Some crew members have said that Roberto Cruz Gomez, El Padre, might still be alive if he had not been wearing a life jacket that tore apart as he was being pulled onboard the *Ducker Tide*.

Crew members also claim that some of the self-inflating life rafts were defective, although Lobb claimed that their inspection certificates were up-to-date. Survivors say that most were not equipped with lights and Very pistols. Many of the rafts were lost when, upon being inflated, their tethers snapped in the hurricane winds and they were blown away before anyone could reach them.

The six divers who were in saturation when

Roxanne passed the first time were very fortunate that the 269 did not sink then. If she had, they most likely would have died either from drowning or from the bends. According to safety experts from McDermott Underwater Services, contingency plans in case the 269 was in jeopardy while men were still in saturation called for the divers to move into the pressurized diving bell, which could then be lowered to the sea bottom. Its cables would be fastened to a buoy floating on the surface. One of the tugs would tow the bell to port, where the men would be transferred to a decompression chamber.

Would this plan really have worked in the face of Roxanne's 35-foot waves? Ray Pepperday, who was intimately familiar with the equipment, did not think that a tug could lift the 15-ton diving bell in hurricane-fed seas. Even if it had been able to, he didn't believe the bell could safely be towed to Carmen or another port. Helicopter transfer of the bell ashore would also have been impossible because of the copter's inability to carry that much weight or endure that much wind. Finally, even if the tug or one of the supply boats had been ordered to attempt to tow the bell to port, that would have left only two vessels to rescue everyone else. Three boats were hardly able to do it.

After Roxanne's first pass, according to diving

superintendent Chuck Rountree, he twice radioed Ed Burgueno, McDermott's diving liaison in Carmen, seeking permission to bring the entire diving contingent ashore. Rountree said that he wanted the six divers who had undergone emergency decompression checked by a hyperbaric physician, rather than trusting the doctor on the barge, who had no special training in diagnosing and evaluating problems resulting from accelerated decompression. Also, Rountree thought that the 269 was no longer safe and he did not want any of his men to stay onboard. Prior to Roxanne's return, a high-speed crew boat could have reached the barge in three hours. Actually, for a short while between Roxanne's first and second appearance, there was a crew boat alongside the barge. Nevertheless, Rountree said that his request was denied and that Burgueno ordered the entire dive crew to remain onboard so that they could complete the remaining work as soon as the 269 could be towed back to the work site. Burgueno says he doesn't remember Rountree ever asking him for permission to bring the diving group ashore, nor does Lobb recall such a request.

One question a mariner might ask is why the two tug captains, if they realized that Roxanne was a danger both to the 269 and to their own vessels and men, didn't simply tow the 269 into Carmen when they had the opportunity—regardless of what C.C.C.'s Lobb or Perot dictated.

Normally, a tug captain has the authority, indeed the responsibility, to safeguard *both* the tug and the tow. Usually a towed craft, most often a barge, is unmanned. In cases where the towed vessel has its own captain, the tug's captain normally maintains overall authority. In this instance, however—in the view of Washington State admiralty attorney Lynn Bahrych—because foreign-flag vessels (the *Captain John* and the *Seabulk North Carolina*) were towing a vessel of Mexican registry (the 269) in her own territorial waters with a Mexican captain onboard, the 269's captain would have overall authority—unless some agreement between the tugs' owners and C.C.C. stipulated otherwise.

And indeed a 1991 agreement between C.C.C. and North Bank Towing did clarify this point. North Bank's tugs (including their chartered *North Carolina*) were themselves *chartered* by C.C.C., and with that charter was transferred authority over and responsibility for both the tug and the supply boat. If the *Captain John* or the *Carolina* had been lost or damaged or their crews injured or killed owing to C.C.C.'s insisting on a hazardous course of action, the captains could have protested. If their formal protests were later upheld in court, the company and/or the crews would have been compensated by C.C.C. Captains Trosclair and Cassel (and their crews) were not very happy about C.C.C.'s insistence on riding out Roxanne at sea, but there was nothing they could do about it.

Another subject that must be discussed is how the sinking affected the survivors. What, if any, repercussions did they experience after their ordeal? Post-traumatic stress disorder, or PTSD, is the long-term psychological and physiological effect of a severe trauma. Aphrodite Matsakis, Ph.D., former clinical coordinator for the Vietnam Veterans' Outreach Center in Maryland, in her book *Post-Traumatic Stress Disorder: A Complete Treatment Guide,* states that PTSD can strike combat vets; concentration camp survivors; rape, torture, and crime victims; abused women and children; and survivors of vehicular accidents and natural catastrophes. All these groups have been in situations of grave danger in which they were helpless. Sufferers are likely to experience nightmares and insomnia, depression, flashbacks they can't block out, anxiety, and often drug or alcohol addiction. PTSD can affect the victim's employment possibilities, personal relationships, and even his or her ability to cope with the simplest aspects of day-to-day living.

Dr. Matsakis goes on to say that although PTSD first became known to the public as "shell shock" suffered by some World War I soldiers, its recorded incidence dates back to the ancient Greek historian Herodotus, who wrote after the battle of Marathon in 490 B.C. that an Athenian soldier, after witnessing a comrade die next to him, suffered permanent blindness without any wound. World Wars I and II, then Korea and Vietnam, opened people's eyes to the psychic horrors of war. Less well known are the similar effects, now well documented, experienced by women and children after repeated sexual and/or physical abuse. The study of PTSD, or traumatology, is a relatively new area of psychology; PTSD was only classified in the DSM (*Diagnostic and Statistical Manual*), the diagnostic and psychological classification authority, in 1980.

Very few 269 survivors suffered long-term physical injuries, but many claim to have experienced PTSD to the point where their personal lives or their employability or both have been threatened. Perhaps the most serious claims are those of Victor Diaz. The lead dive tender not only underwent the traumas of being on the sinking barge and in the sea, but also witnessed at close range a compatriot's disintegration in a rescue vessel's propellers and the victim's severed head bobbing up in front of him.

Since the sinking Victor has, according to Dr. David Mielke, the Tulane University Hospital psychiatrist who testified on his behalf in his lawsuit, "become a shell of what he once was." Dr. Mielke said that Victor is a nonfunctioning member of society, able neither to work nor to attend school regularly. Victor described his condition to me: "I have panic attacks—flashbacks where I'm underwater and where everything turns dark—and, good God, this [is] during the day and, hell, this is the worst: when that head bobs up in front of me. It cripples me basically. Sometimes it's triggered by rain. Then what I do is just lock myself indoors."

According to Victor, the panic attacks, besides fostering uncontrollable nervousness, usually produce headaches and sometimes blistering of the skin on his fingers. Often he can't watch movies. Mostly he just stays in the house. Because his PTSD is so severe, he has developed what psychiatrists call dissociative syndrome, one of whose symptoms is the inability to control the body. Therefore he can't drive a car.

Nor, Victor says, are his nights free of agony. Almost every night he is afraid to go to sleep because his nightmares are so frequent and so severe that he wakes up gasping. He said, "Every night the dreams and the scenario repeats itself. So I have lived it every day for the past almost six years. There's not a night that [goes] by that I can honestly say that I slept perfectly well; there might be one in a 365-day year."

I asked Victor what effect his nightmares and panic attacks have on him. "I cannot describe it to you," he answered. "It's beyond control. I used to have a 9 mm [automatic]. It was to the point where I'd had enough. McDermott had won. I was not going to fight it. I could not live through this hell again, so I took the 9 mm and I had cocked it. I had put it in my mouth and I was about to pull the trigger. But you know, a lot of men died. A lot of good people perished. And these sons of bitches were not going to get away with it. So I turned on the hot water in the bathtub, the shower, and I basically scalded myself. I put the gun away. I finally got rid of it. But there's been a few times that I came really close to pulling the damn [trigger]."

Though Victor takes what his wife describes as a "pharmacy of [prescribed] medicines," she says they don't stop the flashbacks, panic attacks, or nightmares, but just dull them. Victor receives weekly outpatient treatment at a veterans hospital. The psychiatric nurse-practitioner who sees him has had twenty-six years' experience working with PTSD sufferers, both in the military and in VA hospitals. She said, "Victor is one of the worst cases I've seen in twenty-six years, and that includes POW and concentration camp survivors. Every day he lives in hell.

Every day he grieves over the men who died. Every day he thinks of drowning in that sea. Every day he thinks of the company who let this happen once before and knew this storm was coming and didn't do anything to save its men." She continued, "There's no cure [for him]. There's no, like, having surgery and having it taken out. At present he's totally dysfunctional. We are just trying to teach him to cope, not to kill himself, and to get some enjoyment from life."

According to Dr. Mielke, Victor's prognosis is poor.

Many of the 269's survivors, as fearful as they may be, have had to go to sea again because offshore work is the only occupation they know and because they have families to support and bills to pay. Several say they just cannot, will not, go back out, and some of these men and their families are on the verge of bankruptcy. The Mexican survivors are in the worst predicaments. Their financial safety nets were generally meager to begin with, and their difficulties finding other jobs were more pronounced. Also, many of the Mexican crewmen were not seafarers and had never experienced a hurricane at sea— before they experienced three hurricanes in the course of a month. Thus they may have suffered, on average, far more severe PTSD repercussions than the Americans onboard. Skeptics will ask how it may be proven that these men are really suffering from PTSD. Dr. Matsakis indicated that a battery of available tests can convincingly demonstrate whet her someone is experiencing a certain level of post-traumatic stress disorder. One of the plaintiffs' attorneys says that two psychiatrists testifying for McDermott said in depositions that they did not believe the men suffered severe levels of PTSD.

So, how much have the survivors been offered by the companies, how much have they received—and how much are they likely to get?

According to a number of the divers, each member of the twenty-man American dive crew was offered $75,000 by McDermott just after the accident if he agreed not to sue. About half took the offer, but most of those returned the money when they realized that they might not ever be able to work at their old jobs again and therefore that they should seek much more than the amount offered. Four of them and a few of the other American employees on the 269 have settled for between $300,000 and $1 million. Ten other Americans, including Chuck Rountree, Tim Noble, Roy Cline, Rozy, Mitch Pheffer, and Victor Diaz, have not been able to settle with the companies and expect to go to court sometime in the near future.

The situation with the Mexican employees is, as

one might expect, pitiful. Many of the Mexican crewmen who are suing say that initially C.C.C. offered them next to nothing, the peso equivalent of a few hundred dollars. When some threatened to sue, they were offered P10,000, or about $1,100—and jobs—if they did not sue. Nearly all refused. On March 7, 2000, four and a half years after the sinking, the Ciudad del Carmen newspaper reported that C.C.C.'s majority owner, C.F.C., still had not paid the Mexican survivors and the families of those who died. C.C.C. had offered to send the sons and daughters of the deceased to college. So far the company has not kept its promise. According to Charles Musslewhite, a Houston attorney who, along with a few other attorneys, represents most of the crew, the suing Mexicans have received no satisfaction in their own country and are suing in Texas. Musslewhite says the Texas State District Court agreed to hear the case on the basis that the 269 was partly American-owned and that since there are such great injustices in the Mexican legal system, the men probably had no recourse there.

Some of the most disabled by PTSD say that they may never be able to work again. Victor Diaz's attorneys are asking for $2,340,000 for lost wages, past and future, and for medical treatment. Payment for his suffering would be on top of that. This figure will probably be the maximum amount requested by the men's attorneys, other than for settlements with the families of the dead.

The Mexican crewmen will receive far less than the Americans because the Texas court would only hear the case under Mexican law, which does not recognize awards for suffering from PTSD. Unless a settlement is reached, their case will be heard within a year or two.

In retrospect, it seems clear that Lobb and Perot should have had the 269 towed into a safe port. Their argument (in depositions) was that the port of Carmen's channel was too shallow for the 269 with her 19-foot draft. The 269 had entered that bay at least once in the past. Also, the old *Mega Dos,* with a draft nearly as deep as the 269's, had been towed in prior to Roxanne and was towed out again five days later. In any case, the port at Dos Bocas had sufficient depth and would have been reachable if the 269 and her tugs had set out early Saturday evening. The crew members will certainly argue that the $54,000 per day in lost payments from Pemex was the major, if not the only, consideration in C.C.C.'s decision not to tow the 269 in. Richard Lobb, however, has testified that he was not aware of the financial consequences of bringing the barge in to port rather than weathering the storm.

An interesting footnote to the story is that in July 1996, nine months after it sank, the 269 was refloated by Smit International, the world's largest marine salvage company, and towed 40 miles farther out to sea, where she was *resunk* in very deep water. In the United States, the Coast Guard would have demanded a survey of the vessel once she was raised to determine the reasons for the sinking. This was not undertaken here. McDermott/C.C.C. said that the 269 had been raised and resunk because she was in the shipping lanes and was a hazard to navigation. The attorneys for the plaintiffs have questioned this motivation, and others familiar with the operation raised their eyebrows, pointing out that it would now be impossible to obtain physical evidence of the barge's condition at the time it went down.

Attorneys representing some of the crew have suggested that with $10 million worth of hull insurance covering the ancient 269, she was worth more to C.C.C. on the ocean bottom that afloat. Nearing the end of her useful life, she would soon be worth only her value as scrap metal. Also, the attorneys charged that the American Bureau of Shipping inspectors who periodically surveyed the 269 so that she could be insured had failed in their duties. However, the attorneys did not pursue either of these avenues, believing that charges already leveled at C.C.C. and

McDermott were sufficient to further their clients' interests. As a result, it has never been determined whether these allegations had merit. It must be said, however, that there is absolutely no evidence that the barge was deliberately sunk, and the locations of the leaks strongly suggest that it was not.

While I was not able to talk to a spokesman for C.C.C. or its parent company, C.F.C., a statement was received from the president of C.F.C. and is presented in the Appendix. C.F.C. says, among other things, that the Mexican government investigated the accident and found that it was due to an Act of God. It seems likely that the company would place responsibility for the decision to weather the storm at sea on Lobb and Perot. Although Perot claimed to have no memory of taking part in the decision to ride out the storm, others recall his involvement in the numerous conversations throughout the days preceding Roxanne I and II. As the barge superintendent, Lobb could have insisted that the 269 be towed into safe anchorage prior to Roxanne's first arrival, and in retrospect, even he admits he *should* have insisted on towing her in prior to Roxanne II. "By hindsight," Lobb said in his deposition, "now that I know where the storm went, we could have went to a port. . . . We wouldn't have sunk if we got into Dos Bocas. . . . But I didn't have a crystal ball. I couldn't see that far ahead." At least Lobb put his life on the line along with the others on the barge.

C.C.C. had been lucky that the 269 had survived hurricanes in the past, and it was counting on the barge to survive again. Whether a desire to save money played a part in C.C.C.'s actions, as the plaintiffs have argued, may eventually be decided by a court. Witnesses for the company have asserted that money was not a factor.

And what of the responsibility of McDermott, and Offshore Pipelines, Inc., for the 269 disaster? McDermott has disclaimed any responsibility, for several reasons. First, it has said, the majority interest in C.C.C. was owned by a Mexican corporation which controlled and operated C.C.C.; McDermott owned only 49 percent.* Second, the barge's captain and superintendent were C.C.C. employees, and C.C.C. alone was responsible for the barge's movement.

At least one court has ruled that McDermott was not legally responsible for the alleged unseaworthiness of the 269, since the vessel was owned and operated by C.C.C. However, the Louisiana First

---

*When Offshore Pipelines, Inc., formed C.C.C. with their Mexican counterpart, C.F.C., Mexican law required the Mexican partner to own 51 percent of the business. When the North American Free Trade Agreement between the United States and Mexico went into effect in 1994, this requirement was eliminated.

Circuit Court of Appeals agreed with the trial court that McDermott was responsible for the safety of the dive crew. In reviewing the trial court's decision in a suit brought by one of the members of the dive crew, Kristian Nielsen, the circuit court ruled that McDermott had a policy in place to evacuate the dive crew in hazardous circumstances and had the authority to evacuate them. Its failure to do so in the case of the 269 was negligent.

Further, in depositions in the crew members' lawsuits, McDermott's marine superintendent for the Gulf of Mexico, Captain Hans Fuhri, testified that McDermott had a set of "severe-weather guidelines" which its entire worldwide fleet used to protect it from hazardous weather. In the Gulf of Mexico, if a storm approached within a thousand miles with even *less* than hurricane-force winds, all of the company's vessels would pick up anchor and sail, or be towed, to the nearest safe port. While Roxanne was still on the eastern side of the Yucatan Peninsula and while C.C.C. was trying to decide whether and where the 269 should ride out the hurricane, McDermott vessels operating off the U.S. Gulf Coast—500 miles *farther away* from Roxanne—were already being towed toward safe harbors.

Captain Fuhri further testified that, indeed, the 269 should have been towed to a safe port and that if he had known of the barge's existence, he would have made sure that at least McDermott's men were removed from the vessel. Fuhri's testimony provides further evidence that McDermott, even though it was the minority partner in C.C.C., had the authority to protect its men.

Whatever is eventually determined in this case, it is clear that in many Third World companies lives are risked and sacrificed for less than the $54,000 a day at stake here. Should this be a surprise? Not in countries where there is no lack of bodies to fill job openings, and laws protecting workers and making large corporations pay for negligence are weak or nonexistent.

In most of the Third World, taking a safe route while losing the company money is not rewarded; it is frowned upon and often results in replacement of the responsible employees. Third World corporate policy often dictates that risks be taken, even if those risks might put lives in jeopardy. Insurance covers damage to equipment; loss of life is a risk that workers are expected to take. This mentality, coupled with the knowledge that a company will lose very little in local courts in less-developed countries, allows top-level management to discourage its employees from emphasizing safety and it invites disasters to occur.

Seamen familiar with the working conditions in the Third World were also not surprised to hear the allegations by the crew of the 269 regarding the state of the lifesaving equipment and even the barge itself. Although they cannot speak about C.C.C. specifically, they do say that many companies seem to believe that there is little to gain and money to lose by replacing life jackets, making sure life rafts are ready to deploy, and spending an hour a week on rescue drills. In the eyes of Third World corporate management, potential loss of life and human concerns seldom seem to be part of the equation. Even if all of the crew's allegations about the condition of the 269 are true, she was probably no better and no worse than thousands of other commercial vessels sailing under Third World flags.

So what can be done to protect workers throughout Mexico, Asia, and other areas where workers' lives are sometimes viewed as of little value? One high standard of safety should be used by American companies anywhere in the world, regardless of whether they are conducting operations themselves or are in partnership with a foreign corporation. If American companies and other developed nations' companies that are minority partners cannot guarantee both their own and their foreign employees the highest standard of safety, they should not enter into

Carmen (an *abastecedor* is a purveyor or caterer). The company is a shipping agency that provides crews and supplies for North Bank and other vessel operators. Eulalio Zapata, one of the unsung heroes of the rescue, has had jobs offshore, mostly as mate, but is presently out of work.

And how are the survivors faring? Gustavo Zaldivar, the storesman who worked with El Padre, resumed working for C.C.C., now Global Offshore, and is a storekeeper on another barge. He and his wife worry continually that what happened to the 269 will occur again. Marco Polo, the diver, was unemployed for more than a year and then was rehired by Global. At present he works as a diver for another company. Raul Salabania Acosta, the valve tech, has worked at a succession of temporary jobs on and off shore. Luis Domingo de la Riva has not been able to find any steady employment since the sinking. According to his attorney, he suffers from severe PTSD and takes medications daily.

According to Charles Musslewhite, some of the Mexican survivors he represents went back to C.C.C. asking for jobs after the 269 went down. They were among the more than 170 Mexican crewmen who were suing the company to receive compensation for their suffering during and after the sinking. They were told, "If you don't want anything from this company [compensation], we will give you a job. If you continue with the court [the lawsuit], forget about a job." Most have nevertheless persevered in their claims.

While the Americans fared better than the Mexicans, they too have suffered. Ray Pepperday is still an instrument (diving) technician, but he works mostly onshore now. Every time he has to go back out on a barge to spend a few weeks servicing gauges, regulators, and decompression chambers, he looks carefully at the barge's condition, layout, and safety equipment, to prepare himself just in case.

Lenn Cobb figures he will always be a diver, but since the 269 incident, he has changed. Working mostly on barges in the Gulf, he constantly checks the weather forecasts. In the summer of 1998 when Lenn was working on a barge off the Texas coast, the barge crew created a bogus weather forecast predicting a hurricane's arrival right over them. Lenn says, "I got on everybody's butt. 'Come on, it's time to pick up anchors and get the hell outta here!'" Finally the barge captain told the crew, "Hey, that's enough. Y'all have screwed with this guy's head enough."

Some men have found work ashore. Opie now successfully sells life insurance in New Orleans.

Tim Noble is a project manager for a company producing remotely operated undersea vehicles. However, he has seen his twenty-five-year marriage collapse. His ex-wife told him that the sinking changed his personality. Lee Lloyd says he was informed by dive physicians that, indeed, the accelerated decompression during Roxanne's first approach had caused neurological problems and as a result he can never again dive deeper than 30 feet. Thus he has had to give up his only real passion, diving. Both Lee and his wife, Renee, feel that he is not as easy-going as he once was. He loses his temper more often and is more irritable. Lee is a partner in a small company that does civil and criminal background screening.

Two Americans who say they are suffering from PTSD are Ron Rozmarynoski and Kevin Dumont. Though Rozy had not been on the 269's sister barge that sank in the South China Sea four years before the 269 went down, he was one of the first rescuers on the scene and helped to recover both survivors and bodies. That experience, together with his own on the 269, has caused emotional damage from which he says he has not recovered. He is not working. Kevin is still being treated for post-traumatic stress disorder. He hopes to go back to school, perhaps to study photography. He stresses that he will *never* go back to sea. Victor Diaz says he is still totally incapacitated and lives with the faint hope that he will eventually see better days.

In 1996, McDermott's interest in C.C.C. was sold to Global Offshore, which in turn is a division of the huge construction conglomerate Brown and Root—the company that initially built and operated *DLB-269*. Global sold its 49 percent of C.C.C. back to C.F.C., the Mexican parent company, in 1999. J. Ray McDermott continues to be a major operator in offshore platform and pipeline construction and installation. The diving branch, which amounted to a very small part of its overall business, was sold to Horizon Offshore Contractors and just recently was resold to Cal-Dive International. Joe Perot retired but still lives in Mexico. Richard Lobb is there too. He no longer wishes to go to sea but is chief of operations for a large offshore contractor in the Ciudad del Carmen area. Lobb makes sure his vessels are the first towed in to shelter preceding major storms. The whole industry there seems to have learned a lesson from the sinking, and safety has become more than an empty slogan. Also, every October 15, work on offshore barges stops for a minute of prayer and reflection for those who didn't come back, and someone usually tosses a handful of flowers on the water.

* * *

Finally, the 269 herself lies peacefully on the bottom of the Gulf of Mexico, some 70 miles off the Yucatan coast, in silent testimony to the fate that befell her and her crew. She is home, now, only to the creatures of the sea.

AFTERWORD

Because of the ongoing litigation, there were a number of men I could not interview, including Richard Lobb, Joe Perot, and Ed Burgueno. Perhaps they would not have talked to me in any case, though Richard Lobb told me that he wanted to provide his side of the story but could not while the lawsuits were still going on. Nor could I question McDermott or C.F.C. However, please see the companies' statements in the Appendix.

Appendix

❧

STATEMENTS FROM J. RAY McDERMOTT

AND FROM C.F.C.

J. Ray McDermott, S.A.

1450 Poydras Street
New Orleans, Louisiana 70112-6050

P. O. Box 61829
New Orleans, Louisiana 70161-1829
(504) 587-5300
Fax: (504) 587-6153
Telex: 6821250 JRMC UW

<u>Statement to Michael Krieger</u>
<u>Regarding the DLB 269</u>

The DLB 269 was owned, operated and maintained by CCC Fabriccaciones y Construcciones, a Mexican corporation in which J. Ray McDermott was a minority shareholder as a result of its acquisition on January 31, 1995 of Offshore Pipelines, Inc. (OPI) and OPI's interest in CCC. The majority interest in CCC was owned by Grupo Consorcio de Fabriccaciones y Construcciones, also a Mexican corporation, which controlled and operated CCC.

At the time of the sinking on October 15, 1995, the DLB 269 was working on a CCC contract. The barge's crew and superintendent were CCC employees, and CCC was responsible for the barge's movement before and during hurricane Roxanne. The 20 J. Ray McDermott employees on the barge were divers and associated diving personnel. None were involved in decisions regarding the barge's movement and all survived without significant injury, including the divers who were decompressed.

While we take issue with Chuck Roundtree's statements regarding requests for evacuation, claims by the divers are currently in litigation and we cannot directly address his statements.

J. Ray McDermott owns one of the world's largest fleets of marine construction vessels. Our vessels operate according to rigorous standards for personal safety. Over the past decade, we have made constant strides in improving our safety record, and we maintain one of the best—if not the best—personal safety records in the entire marine construction industry. Our standards were in place on all McDermott vessels in October 1995, but because DLB 269 was not a McDermott vessel, it did not operate under our standards. Subsequent to the sinking, J. Ray McDermott terminated its interest in CCC.

September 18, 2001

Ing. Félix Cantú A.
Presidente
FC-2/Mayo/02-026

May 2, 2002

MR. MICHAEL J. KRIEGER
Fax: (360)376-5380

Mr. Krieger:

In response to your fax dated March 28, 2002, received in my office on April 23, 2002, I simply want to state that the DI,B 269 was issued an A1 Maltese Cross rating, the highest, from the American Bureau of Shipping on September 5, 1995 and was certified seaworthy in all respects at the time of the sinking.

In addition, the sinking was investigated by the Mexican government and they found no fault on the part of CCC or unseaworthiness of the vessel. Indeed, their finding was that the sinking was due to an Act of God.

Regards,

GRUPO CONSORCIO DE FABRICACIONES Y CONSTRUCCIONES, S. A. DE C.V.
M . de Cervantes Saavedra No. 157
11520 México, D. F.
Tel. 5254-0511

Visit
❖ Pocket Books ❖
online at

www.SimonSays.com

Keep up on the latest new
releases from your favorite
authors, as well as author
appearances, news, chats,
special offers and more.

SIMON & SCHUSTER
A VIACOM COMPANY
www.SimonSays.com

Pocket
Books

2381-01